Introduction

I have practiced institutional research for n... years primarily using quantitative methods in generating decision support information. Generally, my use of qualitative methods was more a pragmatic, convenient, alternative reaction to time constraints (interviewing through focus groups instead of using a survey of some sort) rather than a selected methodology based on the question to be answered. And, while these methods seemed to meet my needs, it did not become clear to me how useful qualitative methods could be to increase the strength and usefulness of the information I was creating until as a faculty member I taught a graduate course in qualitative research methods.

My first experience with this course was in a team teaching situation where my colleague had a background in qualitative research. Our first conversation about what should be included in the course quickly turned into a point-for-point debate about the merits of each approach. It was from that first conversation that Ken Borland and I both began to understand that when used as complementary methods, the results of research efforts (particularly assessment and evaluation studies) had the potential to be much more useful. This was particularly true as we discussed mixed methods uses in the creation of decision support information or in the assessment of academic and support programs. During my tenure as a full-time faculty member, I taught the qualitative methods course five times, and through these experiences I have become more comfortable with the methods used by qualitative researchers, how mixed methods approaches can enhance a study, and the knowledge that can be developed.

In part, the genesis of this volume reflects my growth in understanding how qualitative research can enhance the usefulness of traditional quantitative work typically performed in institutional research offices. When used in a complementary fashion, the quantitative approaches allow one to assess **what** the outcomes of a program or process are, while the qualitative methodologies provide the researcher with insights about **why** the outcomes developed as they did.

Richard D. Howard
University of Minnesota

Chapter 1
The Role of Mixed Method Approaches in Institutional Research

Richard D. Howard
University of Minnesota

Kenneth W. Borland, Jr.
East Stroudsburg University

Fundamental to the consideration and use of mixed methodology in institutional research is understanding its purpose within the context of institutional research and its place relative to the two dominant contemporary research paradigms. Therefore, prior to introducing this specific volume, we first discuss the purpose of mixed methodology relative to the "what" and "why" questions institutional researchers address. We then discuss the place of mixed methodologies relative to positivist and constructivist research paradigms.

Answering the "What" and "Why" Questions

The fundamental purpose of institutional research is to create data-based information that supports planning and decision making. Traditionally, the majority of the data used by professionals in institutional research offices has its origin in the operating systems of the college or university or was collected through surveys or other studies. These data typically are quantitative, numerical or readily coded in numerical form. From these data institutional research professionals are able to describe their institutions: student enrollments; faculty counts by rank; ethnic breakdowns, etc.; and the activities and outcomes of academic, research, and service programs and processes. These institutional research functions and quantitative data typically describe "what" has happened. The resulting academic and social outcomes are metrics for measuring progress toward goal attainment, and they tend to reflect information used in summative decision making.

These data, however, do not provide all the information necessary to support formative decisions about the effectiveness or efficiency of the ongoing processes that define the program. In other words, productivity data or those collected and analyzed in quantitative studies do not usually provide information about "why" the status of programs is as it is. Nor do they explain why the outcomes of a process are what they are—good or bad. Information about both the outcomes and why they are what they are provides the decision maker with information that will inform policy formation or adjustment as well as an indicator of the overall success (outcomes) of

Using Mixed Methods in Institutional Research

Edited by
Richard D. Howard

The Association for Institutional Research
Number Seventeen
Resources in Institutional Research

Table of Contents

the program or process. The type of information that addresses the question of "why" is usually qualitative, narrative data within a particular context collected using various interview methodologies or open-ended questions on surveys.

Below is a brief example of how the two methodologies were used to identify and understand a student performance issue by answering both the "what" and "why" questions.

A number of years ago, the institutional research analysts in an office at a large university conducted a study of grading patterns in introductory courses. Reviewing ten years of trend data, it was discovered that the average grade in an introductory biology course had dropped significantly (from a B to a C- level) over the preceding five-year period. This was a course that had traditionally been used by non-science and math majors to meet the core science requirements. From these trend data, the institutional research staff learned "what" had happened in terms of academic performance in the course, but it was not known "why" it happened. Through a series of interviews with the students, department head, and faculty who had taught the course over the previous seven years, information was developed about "why" it happened. In response, the department made changes that resulted in student grades for the course returning to former levels of achievement.

Specifically, the institutional research staff found from focus interviews with the students who had taken the course the previous semester that the faculty teaching the course, contrary to its catalog description, taught the course using calculus-based tools. The department head indicated that new faculty were usually assigned the course, as it gave them an opportunity to teach a course that did not require a great deal of content preparation on their part. When asked about recent hiring, he indicated that the department was building capacity to react to emerging biotech opportunities. In other words, new assistant professors were analytic-research oriented in their training and interests. Their approach to the introductory course was analytic in nature, using math-based tools beyond the skills of most students who were advised to register for the course. To the department head's credit, once the reason for the downward trend in the grades was pointed out, the course content and approach was standardized to reflect its original intent. The

*average grade in the course returned to former levels within
a semester.*

In this example, the staff in the institutional research office used both quantitative and qualitative methodologies, first to identify and describe "what" was happening and second to determine "why." The department head made changes based on what the institutional research staff learned about "why" student grades had fallen significantly over the seven-year period. The impact of the changes was assessed through the quantitative analysis of "what" the grades were in the course during the following semesters.

Two Dominant Research Paradigms

In their text on research methods, Best and Kahn (1998), provide a classic definition of research as "the systematic and objective analysis and recording of controlled observations that may lead to the development of generalizations, principles, or theories, resulting in prediction and possibly ultimate control of events" (p. 18). During the past 40 years, the relevance of classical research conducted to understand human behavior has been questioned; and these "questions" have at times been expressed with emotion (Hedrick, 1994). As described below, the paradigms that govern the use of qualitative and quantitative methodologies, define two opposing worldviews or beliefs of reality or truth that ultimately can not be proven.

Paradigms are the world views that are held by a group of scientists that reflect their beliefs about the nature of reality or truth. In the world of social science research, there are two opposing paradigms. Gliner and Morgan (2000) describe them as Constructivist and Positivist. Broadly, the Constructivist believes that there are multiple realities and that truth is ever changing, dependent on context and the individual (subject and researcher). Positivists on the other hand believe that there is a single reality or truth across time and contexts, and that this truth can be understood through the objective study of independent variables. In the first case, the focus is on humans and "their" understandings of the phenomenon at the time and place of the study; while in the second case, the focus is on variables that define the construct or phenomenon under study, with the findings able to be generalized to the population.

The implications for research from these beliefs are significant when looked at from a methodological perspective and fundamental purpose. Methodologically, the Constructivist selects the individuals to be studied as they reflect specific characteristics of interest. The intent is to develop hypotheses or theories that would describe the phenomenon understudy and describe in detail what the subjects say, the environment, and the researcher's role. Generalization beyond the population or context understudy is the not the researcher's responsibility, but is ultimately the responsibility of the consumer of the research (Borland, 2001).

The Positivist believes that cause/effect relationships existing in nature can be measured by isolating the impact of demographic and environmental attributes (variables) typically through sampling procedures (Borland, 2001). From the findings, the researcher generalizes, with a level of confidence, to the population from which the sample was selected, thus suggesting a description of the population and predicting behaviors related to the variable studied.

Given the diametrically opposing beliefs about the nature of reality that these two paradigms reflect, it is not surprising that proponents of each camp have argued passionately for their point of view over the years. In the volume "The Qualitative-Quantitative Debate: New Perspectives" edited by Reichardt and Rallis (1994) the arguments for each paradigm are presented within the context of conducting program evaluations. The intensity of the arguments or "paradigm wars" resulted in two research cultures that in essence advocated that the two paradigms and their associated methodologies can not and should not be mixed (Johnson & Onwuegbuzie, 2004).

Building on these notions, paradigms and methodologies should not be thought of as synonyms; nor does the belief in one world view or paradigm demand the use of a particular methodological approach. As is always the case, the appropriate method and form of data collection are dependent on the question that is to be answered by the research. If the intent is to develop a theory or hypothesis, then specific individuals may be selected to study; and both quantitative and qualitative methodologies can be used to create the desired information. If, the intent is to discover and/or describe a trend within a population or to study an attribute of a population, then a representative sample is selected and the trend or attribute is studied, quantitatively or qualitatively, and the results are generalized to the population. From this perspective, the key issue is how the people to be studied are selected—randomly from a defined population or purposefully to reflect a specific characteristic.[1]

The two paradigms and respective research methodologies can be thought of as the extremes of a "research continuum" with the Positivist at one end and the Constructivist at the other. Borland (2001) suggests that "The relationship between qualitative and quantitative research should not be considered in terms of a mutually exclusive dichotomy but rather as a continuum of complementary paradigms within systematic scientific inquiry that, when used in concert, produce complete or useful knowledge" (p. 5). This concept of approaching research is defined as mixed methods research by Johnson and Onwuegbuzie (2004). They further suggest that this approach to creating knowledge may be thought of as a third research paradigm that bridges the "schism between quantitative and qualitative research" (p. 15). Creswell (2005) further discusses mixed methods research as a world view or paradigm in which the pragmatists believe in "what works" for a particular problem and that the researcher should use what ever methods necessary to understand the problem.

It seems that this is a particularly attractive philosophy for those practicing institutional research. One reason is that the theoretical intent of systematic scientific inquiry, which transcends particular research paradigms and methodologies, is to ultimately address all possible "what," "why," and "so what" questions. In a practical sense, the institutional research professional's work is both limited and delimited. She or he is constrained by limited institutional resources of time and money as well as a specific institutional context which is bounded by organizational structures, processes, and values (Howard & Borland, 2001). In reality, the pressure on the institutional research professional is to develop alternatives or answers to questions of decision makers regardless of the restrictions Positivist or Constructivist paradigms might impose.[2]

Creswell (2005) defines mixed methods research design as a "procedure for collecting, analyzing, and "mixing" both quantitative and qualitative data in a single study to understand a research problem" (p. 510). While the use of mixed methods has been around since the early 1930s, it is only within the past couple of decades that it has become an accepted form of research. In this text, Creswell also describes the evolution of mixed methods research over the past 80 years, providing a rationale for why it has only been relatively lately that mixed methods have become an accepted approach to conducting research.

This Volume

For the most part, institutional research has been described as a profession that primarily uses quantitative methods to conduct its work. Over the years, most of the Association's publications have focused on the use of quantitative methods in describing studies and institutional research work. Exceptions to this have included the use of two qualitative methods—focus group interviews and open ended questions in surveys. In this volume, the integrated use of qualitative **and** quantitative methodologies, or mixed methods is explored. Using case studies that describe the use of mixed methods, the authors illustrate the use of qualitative and quantitative data and methodologies to create information that is used to support planning and decision making at four year universities, community colleges, and within a national organization.

With respect to Creswell's (2005) admonition, that conducting mixed methods research it is necessary to understand both qualitative and quantitative research methods, in this volume, we preface the presentation of the mixed methods case studies with discussions of the two methodologies. Carol Trosset (chapter 2) and Rob Toutkoushian (chapter 3) provide an overview of qualitative and quantitative methods. In these chapters, Trosset (qualitative) and Toutkoushian (quantitative) discuss the techniques and analyses used in the methodologies, providing descriptions of the two approaches to creating knowledge. While knowing and understanding the technical aspects of these methodologies are important for conducting institutional research, their strengths and limitations are predicated on the philosophies or paradigms that provide a framework for their use and should also be understood by the researcher. In the following, these paradigms are defined and discussed in terms of their methodological implications and how the use of mixed methods can take advantage of the strengths of both.

In the following chapters, case studies are presented which illustrate the usefulness of mixed methods in planning and decision support activities. It is my hope that for those of you who have not explored the use of mixed methodology these case studies will provide you with "a new paradigm" from which you might study the institution. To those familiar with the use of mixed methodology, these case studies may provide you with more ideas about using mixed methods in institutional research.

References

Best, J. W., & Kahn, J. V. (1998). *Research in education*, (8th ed.) Allyn and Bacon.

Borland K. W. (2001) Qualitative and quantitative research: A complementary balance. In R. D. Howard & K. W. Borland, Jr., (Eds.), *Balancing qualitative and quantitative information for effective decision support, New directions for institutional research, 112*. San Francisco, CA, Jossey-Bass

Creswell, J. W. (2005). *Educational research: Planning, conducting, and evaluating quantitative and qualitative research*, (2nd ed.) Upper Saddle River, New Jersey: Pearson.

Gliner, J. A. & Morgan, G. A. (2000). *Research methods in applied settings: An integrated approach to design and analysis*. Mahwah, New Jersey: Lawrence Erlbaum Associates.

Hedrick, T. E. (1994) The quantitative-qualitative debate: Possibilities for integration, In C. S. Reichardt & S. F. Rallis, (Eds.), *The qualitative-quantitative debate: New perspectives. New Directions for Program Evaluation, 61*. San Francisco: Jossey-Bass.

Johnson, R. B. & Onwuegbuzie, A. J. (2004). "Mixed methods research: A research paradigm whose time has come". *Educational Researcher*, (Vol. 33, No. 7, pp. 14-26). Accessed on 11/2/006 at: http://www.aera.net/ uploadedFiles/Journals and Publications/Journals/ Educational Researcher/Volume 33 No 7/03ERv33n7 Johnson.pdf.

Lincoln, Y. S. & Guba, E. G. (1985) *Natural inquiry*, Newbury Park, CA: Sage.

Endnotes

1. The above has been a very short discussion of a complex issue. Understanding, at a basic level, of the Positivist and Constructivist beliefs about reality and implications for the creation of knowledge is important if one is to understand the strengths and weaknesses of the research methodologies that they use. Gliner and Morgan's (2000) comparison of the two philosophies, within the context of five axioms proposed by Lincoln and Guba might be a good starting point for those unfamiliar with these philosophical perspectives.

2. We recognize that the Constructivists argue that an important contribution of qualitative research is to identify the "meaning" that people give to their experiences or phenomena that they have witnessed. However, this type of knowledge is not often pursued in institutional research.

Chapter 2
Qualitative Research Methods for Institutional Research

Carol Trosset
Hampshire College

Qualitative research methods are highly developed in some academic disciplines, especially cultural anthropology, and are increasingly in demand within institutional research. Like other types of methods, they can be used for a variety of purposes and in the service of a variety of theoretical paradigms. All qualitative approaches involve the collection of the words and thoughts of other people. Some of them also involve the rigorous analysis of these words and thoughts. This article will address both the collection and the analysis of qualitative data, although not every project will need to draw on all the methods described here.

Within the community of quantitative researchers, qualitative methods often remain the object of various popular stereotypes that both restrict their use and diminish their status. I will begin this discussion by bringing these into the open and getting them out of the way. The three most pervasive misperceptions are that qualitative research is (a) non-empirical, (b) subjective, and (c) anecdotal.

What is wrong with these characterizations? First, *empirical* simply means using or based on data, and data come in many different types – including both quantitative and qualitative. Second, *subjective* should refer not to a methodology but to the subject matter of people's internal experiences and perceptions. The stereotype implies that qualitative researchers are simply communicating their own feelings and biases, but there is no reason why this should be the case. On the other hand, treated as a topic, human subjectivity is one possible thing about which a researcher might gather data—and those data are often qualitative, but they may sometimes be quantitative, as when survey respondents are asked to use a Likert scale to quantify their opinions. Third, "anecdotal" refers to a common practice in which one or a few data points are selectively presented as a substitute for an empirically grounded argument. Stories about individuals' experiences are indeed frequently used in this way—and so are isolated statistics, taken out of context.

I submit, then, that if qualitative research *were* non-empirical, subjective, and anecdotal it would be of poor quality, and would probably not deserve to be called *research*. Qualitative methods, however, just like quantitative ones, are based on data that are systematically collected and analyzed. *Qualitative* research simply means that the data are not numbers. Instead, they are usually words, things the people we study have said or written.

One final misperception about qualitative research is that anyone can do it without special training. True, anyone can ask questions and write down people's answers, just as anyone can count things. Neither of these in their naïve form constitutes research. Like quantitative studies, qualitative research requires appropriate project design, data collection methods, and analytical techniques. In what follows, I will describe various processes but will usually not name them, as qualitative researchers and their disciplines use a wide variety of terminologies. The important thing is not what these processes are called, but that they be carried out in ways that increase the quality of the data and the resulting interpretations.

Collecting Qualitative Data

Qualitative data can be gathered in a variety of ways, two of which frequently appear on surveys. Some standard survey questions collect nominal or categorical data, such as religious preference or anticipated major. Categorical data are easily represented numerically and can be manipulated statistically, but the possible responses are discrete entities and any rank order established between them would be arbitrary.

The more visibly qualitative type of survey data are the comments, where people write text responses to open-ended questions. Sometimes these are written in response to a particular question with a specific focus, but often an otherwise numerical survey ends with some *white space* and instructions such as "please write additional comments here." In these latter cases, the comments may refer to almost anything at all.

Other methods of collecting qualitative data involve face-to-face interaction, with the researcher asking questions of the subjects. Interviews are generally conducted one-on-one, and may be more or less structured. In a highly structured interview, the questions have been determined in advance and are asked of each person in the same way. At the other extreme lies the unstructured interview, in which the researcher intentionally elicits information on particular topics but without a prescribed *schedule* of questions.

Focus groups are another popular method of collecting qualitative data. In a focus group, a number of people (often eight to twelve, but the number varies) are "interviewed" together. This may sound like just a more efficient way to interview more people in less time, but it has the added (and sometimes desirable) complication of the members of the focus group responding to each other's comments. An astute focus group leader will gather information not simply on what each participant says, but also on how the participants influence each other's remarks. Sometimes focus groups are designed to be relatively homogeneous with respect to some variable of interest to the researcher, such as junior and senior faculty members, or white students and students of color.

10

Pre-existing texts can form an additional source of qualitative data. For example, college view books could be read as providing data on what institutional qualities they believe their prospective students will value. Or a set of end-of-course evaluation comments could be read, not for information about the quality of individual instructors, but to discover whether a particular population of students believes they are being asked to work too hard or not hard enough.

The choice of data collection methods is usually a trade-off between quantity and quality of data. For example, you can administer a survey to hundreds of people and learn a lot, but you will learn less about any one individual's thoughts and experiences than if you interview that person in depth. On the other hand, in-depth interviewing gathers much detailed information but requires a great deal of time (and, therefore, usually money as well), so it is rarely possible to interview a large number of people.

The choice of data collection methods should, whenever possible, be guided by what you want to find out. There are at least four kinds of circumstances in which interviews or focus groups will be more helpful than surveys.

- When you aren't sure what you want to know.
- When the topic is complex and you aren't sure what questions to ask.
- When you're trying to study people's unconscious assumptions which they may not be able to articulate.
- When you're designing a survey and want to test whether the questions work.

The risk we take when we administer surveys is that the person answering the questions will interpret them differently than we did when we posed them, but that we won't be able to tell this from looking at their answers. In an interview, however, if a person misunderstands the question, or goes off at a tangent, the interviewer can ask immediate follow-up questions and make sure the two people are communicating in ways that further the research. By hearing a range of things that occur to people when a particular question is posed, the researcher can refine that question, or learn that posing a different one would be more useful. In a sense, all of these points indicate that qualitative methods are extremely useful for exploratory research.

Focus groups are a popular method and, as mentioned above, seem like an efficient way to interview more people. There are, however, various circumstances in which interviews are a better technique than focus groups, including the following:

- When the topic is sensitive and people may be reluctant to speak in front of others;

- When you don't want people to influence each other's responses;
- When you aren't sure how to group people to permit effective discussion; and
- If you are better at paying close attention to one person at a time.

Anyone gathering data in these ways should be taking notes. (For focus groups, it usually works better to have one person direct the discussion and a second person take the notes.) Sometimes researchers also make recordings. Whether to do so is a judgment call. On the one hand, tape recordings provide the researcher with a more detailed record of what was said than can be obtained in written notes. On the other hand, transcribing tapes is difficult and takes a very long time. Some individuals will not want to be recorded, and in focus groups, it will be difficult to tell from the tape which person said what.

Whatever data collection method is used, the researcher must answer various design questions, including two in particular: (a) which and how many people should be interviewed, and (b) what questions they should be asked.

The first of these is a sampling question. The answer, as usual, depends on the purpose of the research. It is always good practice to ensure that one's sample includes a range of whatever types of people make up the target population. There are several ways to draw samples. A *random* sample is one in which every member of the population has an equal chance of being selected. Many people erroneously assume that random sampling always results in a group of people who are representative of the population, but this may well not happen unless the sample includes a large percentage of the population. What, after all, does *representative* mean? Answering this question requires deciding what characteristics of the population are important to the researcher, and until we do the research, we can't be sure how to answer that question.

For example, gender and ethnicity are often built into *stratified* samples (which draw separately from particular subgroups within the population). These dimensions are important for sampling, if only because the people for whom we do the studies will wonder whether these qualities make a difference—that is, whether male and female students have different levels of satisfaction, or different levels of involvement in various activities. We might, however, discover that gender does not make a difference to these things, but because we didn't know anything else about members of the population when we drew the sample, we were unable to stratify it on any other basis. Sometimes we can use other information. For example, if a few dozen students are being interviewed about residence life, it would be best to make sure to include some individuals from each residence hall. However, because qualitative studies almost always involve small samples, it is important to be cautious about extrapolating the results to an entire population, or to refrain from doing so altogether. This caution is in order no matter how apparently representative your sample.

Two other sampling strategies are sometimes useful, especially in qualitative research. One is called a *snowball* sample. Snowball samples are obtained by making a few initial contacts and then asking them to refer you to other people who might be willing to be interviewed, or who might have other perspectives. This technique has the advantage that when you approach a new person, you can say you have been referred to them by someone they know. This approach can dramatically increase the number of people who are willing to participate in a study, and used carefully it can result in a very diverse sample. Another type is called a *convenience* sample, which means that we talk with people to whom we have easy access. Convenience samples can be very useful for exploratory research, and for helping to design a study and test interview questions, but it is very important not to extrapolate the results obtained from them without also using other strategies, since the people who are easy to find may have other things in common, such as all taking a certain course or all working for the admissions office—the type of factors that might limit the range of responses we might hear from them.

In designing the questions to be asked in an interview or focus group, it is important to remember that what you want to find out is often somewhat different from what you need to ask. For example, the questions you ask must address things the people you interview have knowledge of, such as their thoughts, their immediate behavior or direct experience, or their reactions to some information or event. Though flawed, one widely used question is found on some end-of-course evaluations: when students are asked whether the professor is knowledgeable about the subject matter. Students can tell us whether the professor *appeared* knowledgeable, and whether the material was clearly presented, but since by definition students are not experts in the subject matter of the course, they cannot give us useful information on whether or not the professor *is* knowledgeable.

Another potential pitfall in framing questions is to confuse data collection and analysis, and to ask the interviewees to do our work for us. If we want to know what students think about the new distribution requirements, the best practice would be to ask each of a number of students what he or she as an individual thinks and then compile their various opinions in the process of analysis to build up a picture of the population. While it might be useful to ask the members of our sample what they hear from their friends on the subject, asking them "What do students think about the new requirements?" would not be an empirically sound way to build an answer. Likewise in a longitudinal study, we look at change over time by asking the same question repeatedly and documenting if the person's response changes—this gives us better information than asking someone at a late point "how have you changed?"

After questions have been written, it is important to pilot-test or validate them. (Validity addresses the issue of whether the questions actually measure what we think they measure and will be addressed in more detail in a later section.) This is done by posing them to several people who are typical of those in the intended sample. During these pilot interviews, you will discover what things need to be re-worded so that the test subjects understand the question and provide relevant information. These experiments will indicate how to phrase each question so that it reliably captures high-quality data. Once a few people have responded to the questions without any misunderstandings, and you have obtained from them the sort of information you are seeking, then the questions are probably ready for use. It can also be helpful to go over the questions with another experienced researcher, who may be able to imagine pitfalls you have not yet noticed.

There are many skills involved in collecting qualitative data, and they can be learned. They include framing good questions, asking good follow-up questions, being consistent in how questions are asked of different people, being a good and unbiased listener, and keeping oneself and one's opinions out of the conversation. Another way to think about these skills reveals at least three dimensions:

- The intellectual techniques involved in designing both primary and follow-up questions to elicit information, and to notice the complexities or implications of what is being said;
- The emotional techniques involved in creating the right atmosphere, keeping an interview different from a conversation and establishing good rapport while remaining cognitively detached from the experience of the interviewee; and
- The creativity to be able to perceive undesignated material *as data*, which may reveal the existence of an entire un-used data set, or enable you to notice some idea in time to pursue it during the course of an interview.

Qualitative Analysis Step 1 – Developing Categories

Depending on the goal of the study, the collection of qualitative data may or may not be followed by analysis. Some researchers simply want to capture people's expressions of their own experience and help communicate that to an audience. Many audiences like this sort of thing, and the use of direct quotations, even anecdotally, can be very powerful.

However, much qualitative data goes unanalyzed because people are unfamiliar with appropriate analytical techniques. They type up lists of survey comments and stop. Institutions can learn things just from looking at what people said, but much more can be learned if the data are properly analyzed.

What is the point of qualitative analysis? Remember that nominal or categorical data are qualitative (male/female, first-year/sophomore/junior/

senior). They work well for multiple choice survey questions, and can be coded as numbers and analyzed in crosstabs. But survey and interview comments don't come in this form—they're messy. *Qualitative analysis is about taking messy stuff and turning it into categorical data.* It's a data reduction exercise—somewhat like factor and cluster analysis. In this respect, qualitative analysis is similar to analytical work in other fields that identify categories, such as biological taxonomy, paleontology, or linguistics.

Data reduction does not imply that you lose information by reducing it to something excessively simple. In fact, you gain information because you discover how groups of quotations are related to each other. Instead of treating hundreds of comments as separate, you can combine them and relate particularly rich quotes and examples to larger patterns of perception and experience.

A version of this sort of analysis is often done informally and even unconsciously. When people read the lists of survey comments, they often think things like "Wow, a lot of people are complaining about the new requirements." When the categories are sought systematically, the technique is often referred to as content analysis. It essentially consists of taking batches of text, usually survey or interview comments, and sorting them into meaningful categories.

Good categories have certain properties:

- They are neither arbitrary nor pre-determined. If they were pre-determined and there were only one way to sort things, analysis would not be necessary. On the other hand, they need to be grounded in the data such that they are not infinitely variable.
- Good categories are useful; they tell you something you didn't already know.
- Good categories are "right"—which really means they are culturally accurate in some way. There are several ways to check this: (a) they resonate with the experience of members of the culture being described, (b) other research methods result in a similar interpretation, and/or (c) another researcher can come up with similar results.

There may be more than one "right" answer depending on what kind of thing people need to know. That is, you could divide course evaluation comments (a) in a way that helped you identify better and worse teachers, or (b) in a way that told you what aspects of class discussions students liked and which aspects they disliked. But it's important to remember that there are wrong answers. Not every way of looking at a data set is equally valuable or equally accurate.

When I develop a new set of categories, I start by reading through most or all of the data, just to get a sense of what is there. As I read, I ask myself what I want to know, and I start to notice themes. Depending on the complexity of the issue, one reading may not be enough, so I go back and read everything again, this time making a list of different issues or themes. Eventually the list stops growing, and then I work directly with the list, trying to consolidate the items into a manageable number of categories.

One way to do this consolidation is to read the list and decide on some categories, building a classification from the top down. When the data are simple, such as a list of the types of problems students have encountered in their residence halls, this is usually sufficient. The other way is more gradual, beginning by clustering individual pairs of items that appear very similar, without knowing what categories will eventually emerge. When the data are complex, this is a safer approach. The development of categories should be an inductive process—that is, the answers should emerge from the data, rather than being derived from some pre-existing theory. You don't know in advance which issues will be important in answering your question, so it's important to make sure all the data are included in the analysis. Occasionally a single response may deserve its own category because it reflects an idea or perspective that is different from all the others. That's okay; counting how often the different categories are represented in the data comes later.

It's best to start with more categories rather than fewer. You may decide later that two of them are insufficiently different and should be collapsed, but if you combine them too early, it will be extremely difficult to re-separate them.

Most data sets will require making some decisions about what *kind* of categories are most useful. For example, here is a partial list of comments describing various professors, taken from end-of-course evaluations:

- Available,
- Gives clear explanations,
- Unprepared,
- Organized,
- Vague,
- Cares about students,
- Encouraging,
- Patronizing,
- Supportive, or
- Disorganized.

One approach would be to put all the positive comments in one category and all the negative ones in the other, so that "unprepared," "vague," and "patronizing," and "disorganized" would be grouped together in opposition to all the other items. It is possible, however, to develop a more informative set of categories.

Instead of just counting good and bad comments, we could find out *what aspects of faculty behavior* students are perceiving and describing. Taking this approach, we would first combine "organized" and "disorganized," since they refer to the presence or absence of the same quality. Then we would consider whether "unprepared" should be part of the same group (probably), or whether it seems different enough from "disorganized" to merit a separate category (probably not, but maybe). "Gives clear explanations" and "vague" would form a second group. A third would include "cares about students," "encouraging," "supportive," and "patronizing," all of which refer to the emotional dimension of faculty-student interaction. On this short list, "available" would probably deserve its own category. This approach results in a very informative set of categories, but a relatively complicated one, since each category could be manifested in either positive or negative forms.

Following up on the idea that there are wrong answers, note that it would be very difficult to justify creating a category that combined "organized," "unprepared," and "supportive." Even if one person could be described in all those ways, it would not make sense to combine these terms with each other to the exclusion of all the others.

Sometimes your best categories come by combining responses to several different questions. On an end-of-course form, for instance, there might be separate questions asking about the professor and about the classroom activities. Both might elicit comments about the professor, and if so, if would be worth including all those comments in the process of creating categories.

Qualitative Analysis Step 2 – Coding

After developing a good list of categories, the next step is to return to the raw data and code it. *Coding* is the term that refers to the process of identifying which responses belong in which categories. To develop the categories, all responses were treated as an aggregate data set. What mattered then was the variety of content, not which person gave which response. Now, during the coding process, what matters is which category best describes each response. Like the creation of categories, this step requires making judgment calls.

Sometimes a response may fit well into more than one category. If this happens very often, it may be a sign that the list of categories needs to be revised. However, it could indicate that this response should be split into two responses and the two should be coded separately. (Such as: Person X said one thing about the availability of his adviser and a different thing about the value of discussing career goals in an advising session.)

There are usually some comments that don't belong in any category. These should have been ignored while developing the categories themselves, and often read something like "Surveys like this are stupid." They share the quality of providing no useful information about the topic being investigated.

On the other hand, there will occasionally be a comment that belongs as the only member of its own category. The odds are good that most members of a group being interviewed or surveyed will comment mostly on the same things, since they are, after all, being asked about the same things. However, there may have been one insightful person who thought about something different and interesting, or one person who had a unique but relevant experience. This person's comments should be included in the analysis, though it must be noted that only person fell into that category (see the section on mixed methods, below).

Some comments that should provide useful information must be thrown out because they contain insufficient detail and cannot be classified with certainty. It's important not to over-interpret ambiguous comments. These are common on surveys—people write things like "advising" in response to a question like "What should the college change?" You know this indicates some kind of dissatisfaction with advising, but you don't know *anything* about what aspect of advising that student is dissatisfied with. You will be tempted to assume they are referring to some aspect that another student has mentioned, or that you believe to be a problem, but you mustn't do this.

The mechanics of coding can be done in a variety of ways, both low-tech (a print-out of responses and different colored highlighter pens) and high-tech (an Excel spreadsheet with comments in one column, adding categories in a different column). It can also be done as one stage in the use of qualitative analysis software; however, even here, the researcher must do the thinking and make the decisions about how to code each item. The main benefits of the software are obtained later when you want to assemble all the comments on a particular topic or cross-correlate them with categorical information on the respondents.

Once each response has been coded, you then have a categorical variable. At this point, you can do things like count how many responses fall into each category, link the coded responses to other information about the respondents, and even represent them numerically in data sets and do nonparametric statistics.

Both developing categories and coding responses require a variety of analytical skills. General inductive reasoning skills are fundamental. To develop and use good categories, you must be able to stay with the data and not become too imaginative or theoretical. On the other hand, intellectual creativity enables the analyst to see patterns and to notice ideas and connections that have not already been made explicit. It helps to be able to hold large amounts of information and themes in your memory so that you will notice if a pattern or phrase taps into anything else that is part of the study. And it is necessary to be able to detach and stand back from your own feelings and opinions, so that you will notice and be able to work with views and experiences that you find unfamiliar or even unwelcome.

Validity Issues

Qualitative analysis is not susceptible to mathematical proof. It's sometimes described as being more like a legal proof—a preponderance of the evidence that eventually makes a particular interpretation overwhelmingly probable. It's good to have your findings sometimes produce something intuitively obvious, or to replicate something already known from other sources—this is a good confirmation of the validity and effectiveness of your methods. Local knowledge can help you identify relevant issues, but you should sometimes find concepts you hadn't thought of before. If you don't, you may just be replicating your own assumptions and missing things in the data. The best answers tell you something that you didn't know before, and contribute to an understanding of something that is culturally significant. It's always a good sign when thoughtful insiders find your results resonating for them, having what's sometimes described as an "Aha!" experience. However, an interpretation can be true and not receive this response, either because it doesn't overlap with something people usually notice, or because it describes something people don't like about their own culture and would rather not acknowledge.

The whole concept of validity refers to whether the researcher is measuring the thing he or she is trying to measure. Qualitative data are extremely helpful in doing this. Quantitative researchers sometimes check for validity by seeing whether there are statistically significant differences between respondents of different sociological categories (in cases where those categories are not intended to be the object of the research). But what if everyone is misinterpreting a question in the same way? For example, the use of the word *studying* appears to have shifted over time, from referring to all the work a student did for a class to referring just to test preparation. Quantitative data would only reveal that the reported amount of time spent studying had gone down, but qualitative data can provide an explanation for the shift in how the question is interpreted.

Another validity issue has to do with bias. Some people believe it is impossible for a researcher not to be biased. I disagree, and I believe that careful attention to appropriate methodology is a big part of the solution. Still, everyone has opinions (after doing research on a topic if not before) and must guard against letting those opinions influence the collection, analysis, or presentation of data. It is easiest to do unbiased work when:

- You're new to the community you're studying and have no preconceptions;
- You have no personal opinions or investment in the topic and honestly don't care what the answer is; or
- You don't share the basic assumptions of the group you're studying— this makes those assumptions highly visible.

The best way to avoid bias is to be genuinely interested in what other people think. If you cannot set aside your biases on a particular topic, then someone else should do that particular research project. However, it is often possible, with care, to gather and present honestly and accurately data that reflect views not your own. This aspect of data collection and analysis have been discussed briefly above. With respect to reporting results, all kinds of reporting require authors to make judgment calls about what to say. Including everything in some form is one way to limit apparent bias. It helps to include illustrative quotes that describe points of view you disagree with, to give readers the chance to form their own opinions. Another strategy is to use as few adjectives as possible. Adjectives tend to be one place where your own opinions slip into the analysis, as are descriptions of quantities. Phrases like "many people say" can introduce unconscious biases. Using numbers or percents helps to limit this tendency.

On the other hand, the researcher is the expert on the project. In that role, you have some responsibility to make the audience aware of what you see in the data. One caveat: what you, the researcher, see in the *data*—which is highly relevant to your analysis—may not be the same thing as what you, the individual, think about the *issue*—and your thoughts about the issue are usually not at all relevant to the analysis. But if you think you've found something important in the data, telling readers that they ought to notice certain things is not bias, as long as your argument is supported with evidence from the research.

Using Qualitative Methods In Multi-Method Projects

The combination of qualitative and quantitative methods in a single project can be especially powerful. Each approach accomplishes things that the other cannot do, but many topics benefit from the application of both.

Qualitative methods are wonderful for exploratory research and also for obtaining rich ethnographic detail. Listening to what people say about their thoughts and experiences is an excellent way to learn what the issue really is and to think comprehensively about what needs to be studied. The collection of qualitative data can provide a greatly enriched understanding of quantitative categories. For example, a satisfaction survey gathers quantitative data but usually tells us nothing about *why* the respondents are satisfied or dissatisfied. This is one reason why faculty often want end-of-course evaluation forms to include space for comments—because the numeric responses themselves do not provide useful information about what the instructor might want to do differently to be a more effective teacher.

What do quantitative methods have to contribute to qualitative research? On the simplest level, you do sometimes have to *count* when you summarize qualitative data. It's very important to say whether 60 people or 2 people made a particular comment. The more frequently mentioned issues should be emphasized in a report; however, sometimes one or two people say something you know to be very important. In that case, the report should stress and justify the importance of that thing, but should also make it clear how rarely it was mentioned. On the other hand, qualitative studies usually have small sample sizes. Don't report counts if it would give a misleading impression of how representative your data are. Sometimes you only talk to a dozen people, and the only useful conclusion is something along the lines of "we found two different points of view on this subject, and here they are—we don't know how frequently these views are held in the total population."

Here's where a multi-method study can be particularly useful. The qualitative work from which these two points of view emerged can form the basis for a more extensive study using quantitative methods and a large and representative sample. The identification of the two points of view, and the words respondents used to describe and explain them, should be used to design the survey that gathers the larger data set.

Illustrative examples—sometimes known as "juicy quotes"—can be a great asset in presenting qualitative data. They enrich a report and help readers understand what is going on. They can enhance our effectiveness as applied researchers by making a situation feel real to the decision-makers we are trying to reach. However, to avoid just being anecdotal, we should put these examples in the context of the quantitative presentation of the various categories or make it clear that they are simply present as a more detailed description of categories whose frequencies we do not know.

Finally, coding qualitative responses as categorical data permits us to ask and answer questions about whether certain themes tend to come from particular categories of respondents. Statistical techniques like correlations and cluster analyses can greatly enhance the analytical power of qualitative methods once the categorization and coding work has been done.

Related References on Qualitative Research Methods

Bernard, H. R. (1995). *Research methods in anthropology: Qualitative and quantitative approaches.* Walnut Creek: Altamira Press.

Fetterman, D. M. (1989). Ethnography: Step by step. *Applied Social Research Methods Series, Vol. 17.* Newbury Park: Sage Publications.

Handwerker, W. P. (2001). *Quick ethnography.* Walnut Creek, CA: Altamira Press.

Chapter 3
The Use of Quantitative Analysis
for Institutional Research

Robert K. Toutkoushian
Indiana University

Introduction

There are a number of different methods or approaches that could be taken to investigate issues of interest in institutional research. As described in this monograph, these methods are often grouped into two main categories: quantitative and qualitative studies. There is significant disagreement among education researchers as to which approach is best for studying educational phenomena. Researchers have also disagreed with regard to the theoretical paradigms that underlie their approaches to issues. These debates have been fueled, in part, by the recent emphasis by the federal government on funding research projects that use "scientifically-based methods" (*i.e.*, quantitative methods) such as randomized experiments to determine whether education programs and policies are effective at achieving their goals. This has led to fears that the government is becoming increasingly critical of the field of education, and that qualitative research studies in education will be crowded out in favor of quantitative studies.

Historically, the field of institutional research has perhaps relied more heavily on quantitative methods than other education-related areas. Not surprisingly, this is especially true for the data reporting aspects of institutional research. Many institutional researchers have considerable experience working with data on a daily basis. Institutional researchers access and manage data in student, human resource, and finance systems at their institutions, create statistics about the institution from these data, respond to queries from stakeholders for quantitative information, and work with administrators on their campuses to evaluate policies and programs. All of these activities require the manipulation of quantifiable data on various aspects of the delivery of postsecondary education. Many offices of institutional research routinely compile "fact books" and "performance indicators" about their institutions, in which quantitative data are used to describe their institution, compare it to others, and determine how the institution is changing along various dimensions.

Researchers who use quantitative methods in their work believe that there are causal relationships between particular factors of interest, as shown in Figure 1.

The quantitative researcher begins with a variable (y) such as student academic performance, faculty satisfaction, or institutional reputation that

Figure 1
Diagram of Causal Nature of Education Phenomena

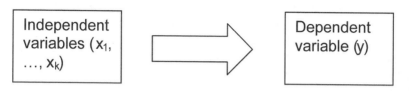

he or she would like to explain. A model is then specified which consists of a set of factors $(x_1, ..., x_k)$ that are believed to have an effect on y based on educational theories. Note that the researcher specifies a direction of causality between factors that may or may not exist. The task of the quantitative researcher is to then obtain measures of the dependent and independent variables and determine if the evidence can refute or support the predictions of theories.

Unlike disciplines in the hard sciences, where hypotheses can be tested more precisely in a laboratory setting, it can be very difficult to implement similar randomized experiments in higher education research. Accordingly, statistical methods are used to obtain evidence to test conjectures about these relationships. The goal of quantitative analysis in institutional research is to uncover evidence about these causal relationships, and then use this information to evaluate or refine institutional policies. Table 1 provides some examples of the types of causal models that an institutional researcher might use for a quantitative study.

Table 1
Hypothetical Examples of Causal Models for Institutional Research

Problem	Data	Dependent Variable	Independent Variables
Which students are most likely to accept admissions offers from a university?	Students who applied to a given university and were admitted	$y = 1$ if admitted student enrolled at the university, 0 otherwise	Measures of student academic ability, distance from university, family characteristics, ability to pay
Are faculty paid differently based on their gender and race/ethnicity?	Faculty members at a given institution in a particular year	y = annual salary for each faculty member	Measures of faculty productivity, years of experience, departmental affiliation, gender, race/ethnicity
How can an institution increase its student graduation rate?	Institutions that have tracked cohorts of students over the same time period	y = percentage of students at each institution who graduated within six years	Measures of the academic quality of the student cohort, price of attendance

To illustrate this approach, suppose that a quantitative researcher were asked by her university president to help the institution understand how students make decisions about where to attend college. A quantitative researcher might begin with human capital theory to posit that a student's college destination is affected by a series of factors such as family income, student ability, gender, and so on. The analyst would then obtain data on these factors from a subset of students and apply statistical methods to determine whether and how these factors affect student choice in the larger population, and then use this information to make recommendations to the president on their financial aid policies.

In this chapter, I explore in greater detail how quantitative methods can be used in institutional research. I begin by describing the nature of quantitative data—what it is and where it can be found. I then turn to the methods that are typically used to collect quantitative data, and conclude by reviewing approaches for analyzing quantitative data. My goal is to help the reader understand the general approach used in quantitative analyses, the flexibility and utility of this approach, and how it can be used for institutional research purposes.

Nature of Data for Quantitative Analyses

Quantitative methods seek to examine the patterns in data or the relationships among variables. The variables used in such analyses are usually numeric, although they may be either quantitative or qualitative in nature. What is the distinction? Generally speaking, qualitative data refer to variables that are categorical measures. These would include factors such as a student's gender and race/ethnicity, a faculty member's departmental affiliation, and an institution's geographic location and Carnegie classification. What identifies these factors as qualitative in nature is that the possible values for each factor (for example, male, Hispanic, Economics, Indiana, Research Extensive) represent categories or groups and are not numerical measurements. In contrast, the values for quantitative variables are numerical and are measurements rather than simply labels for categories. Examples of quantitative data that are encountered in institutional research would include a student's GPA and SAT score, a faculty member's publication count and years of experience, and an institution's retention and graduate rate. In each instance, the possible values for these factors are numeric and the numerical values are measurements of something.

Despite its name, quantitative research methods can be used to examine both quantitative and qualitative data. However, most quantitative applications require that variables with categorical values first be transformed into new variables with numerical values. The most common way of accomplishing this is to apply an assignment rule to the qualitative data to create dichotomous (dummy) variables. For example, suppose that the variable G has two values for gender: male and female. An assignment rule might be devised such as $F = 1$ if G = female, otherwise $F = 0$. The new variable F can now be used in a variety of quantitative methods even though the underlying variable is a qualitative measure. A similar approach can be used for creating dummy variables when there are multiple categories for the qualitative measure, such as with a faculty member's departmental affiliation.

Methods of Collecting Data for Quantitative Analyses

There are a variety of ways that data can be obtained for quantitative studies in institutional research. The first source of data is institutional databases. Institutions collect significant amounts of information on students, faculty, staff, and revenues and expenditures and store them in what are often referred to as legacy or information systems. These large databases were not designed for research purposes, but rather to assist the institution in fulfilling its day-to-day operations. Student information systems, for example, typically contain detailed records on the academic progress of its students for the purpose of conferring degrees. Human resource systems contain information on faculty and staff that are needed to process salary and benefit payments. Finally, financial information systems are used to track details on receipts and expenditures for the university and meet the institution's fiduciary responsibilities. These systems can, however, be used for institutional research purposes provided that thought is given to the type of information to retrieve from each system and the definitions of variables used for each. For example, a salary equity study could be conducted by retrieving data from the human resources information system on faculty in a given year, or a retention study could be performed with data on a cohort of freshmen drawn from the student information system.

Data for quantitative analyses can also be obtained through special studies at the institutional level. Institutional researchers may survey students and faculty to obtain information on various factors of interest to their institutions. Similarly, institutions may contract out with groups such as the National Survey of Student Engagement (NSSE) to collect this type of information. These provide another source of valuable data that can then be used by institutional researchers for analytical purposes.

A third source of data for quantitative analyses is national databases on students, faculty, and institutions. Perhaps the largest entity responsible for such databases is the National Center for Education Statistics (NCES). The NCES databases are of two primary forms. The first represent data that are compiled from information submitted by institutions as part of their federal requirements. These would include the various Integrated Postsecondary Education Data System (IPEDS) surveys on institutional characteristics, finance, enrollments, fall staff, and employees by assigned position. This information can be used by institutional researchers for quantitative analyses comparing institutions on a variety of measures, or for augmenting other datasets with information at the institutional level. The second form of data collected by NCES is from surveys of students and faculty. The National Survey of Postsecondary Faculty (NSOPF), for example, has been conducted periodically to survey random samples of faculty nationwide and collect detailed information on their compensation, work history, and personal characteristics. Student level surveys such as High School and Beyond (HS&B), Baccalaureate and Beyond (B&B), and National Longitudinal Study of the H.S. Class of 1972 (NLS-72) are examples of longitudinal surveys that follow groups of students over time to observe their experiences—educational and otherwise—after high school and college.

Approach to Quantitative Analyses

I now turn to the ways in which institutional researchers can conduct quantitative analyses of higher education data. Quantitative studies rely on statistical analyses as the means for drawing conclusions about educational phenomena. In a statistical analysis, one begins by identifying a parameter of interest and the relevant population represented by the parameter. The population is the entire group of objects that could be examined in the study. For example, an institutional researcher might be interested in learning the average IQ of all freshmen at the institution. In this case, the unknown parameter of interest is the average IQ of all freshmen, and the population is the set of all freshmen at the institution. While the analyses could be conducted by obtaining information on all items in the population, this may not be feasible because of the size of the population and the cost of obtaining this information. Accordingly, the population parameter is not known and must be estimated. In a statistical study, a subset, or sample, of items is drawn from the population and the results studied to draw conclusions about the unknown population parameter.

The statistics that are obtained from the sample are referred to as random variables, because the value for the variable is not known prior to the sample being drawn and can vary from sample to sample. For example, suppose that the average IQ score of freshmen at a given institution is 110, and a sample of 50 students is drawn at random from the student population. One would expect the average IQ score of the 50 students to be 110, but the actual average for this particular sample could be higher or lower. Furthermore, the mean for the first sample of 50 students may be different from the mean of another sample of 50 students drawn from the same population.

Quantitative researchers use hypotheses tests in these situations to draw conclusions about conjectures (hypotheses) for the unknown population parameter. Every hypothesis test consists of three main steps:

1. Determine the null and alternative hypotheses;

2. Identify the appropriate test statistic and its critical value(s).
3. Calculate the test statistic and compare the value to the critical value(s).

The null hypothesis is the value of the population parameter that the researcher assumes is true, and the alternative hypothesis is what must be true if the null hypothesis is false. For example, "The Earth is round" and "The Earth is not round" are two conjectures that could be used in a hypothesis test because one of them must be true when the other is false.

The test statistic is the particular estimator that will be calculated from the sample. Each test statistic has its own distribution which describes the set of possible values for the estimator and their associated probabilities. Some of the commonly used test statistics in institutional research applications include the normal distribution, student t-distribution, binomial distribution, Chi-square distribution, and F-distribution. The distribution is then combined with the researcher's choice of significance level to identify the critical values for the hypothesis test. The critical values represent the maximum limit(s) for the test statistic. When the calculated value of the test statistic exceeds the critical value(s), the evidence is said to be so strong that the researcher can safely reject the null hypothesis and conclude that the alternative hypothesis is correct.

Quantitative researchers assert that hypothesis tests are necessary because in most real-life situations the analyst does not know the value of the statistic for the entire population. In the earlier example, the analyst may not know the average IQ score of all freshmen, and thus does not know what to expect for the sample of 50 students. In a hypothesis test, the analyst would specify a guess, or hypothesis, about what the average IQ score would be for all freshmen. A sample of students is then taken from the population. The analyst then computes the average IQ score for students in the sample (*i.e.*, the sample statistic), and determines how far this value is from what would be expected when the null hypothesis is true. If the sample statistic is not equal to the assumed population parameter, then either (a) the assumption about the population parameter is correct and the sample is not representative of the population, or (b) the assumed value for the population parameter is incorrect. Note that as the distance between the sample statistic and the assumed population parameter increases, it is less likely that (a) is true.

One way to think about hypothesis testing is that it is similar to how legal cases are tried in the United States. When a defendant is charged with a crime and brought to court, it is not known for certain whether the defendant is guilty or innocent. Similarly, in statistical studies it is not known for certain whether the null hypothesis is true or false. The trial proceeds by assuming that the defendant is innocent until proven guilty, just as the hypothesis test assumes that the null hypothesis is true until proven false.

The prosecution collects evidence and presents this to the judge and jury, who then determine if the evidence is so strong that they can conclude that the defendant is guilty "beyond a reasonable doubt." Likewise, the statistician collects data from a sample and uses this as evidence to prove beyond a reasonable doubt that the null hypothesis is false. Finally, in each instance there is the possibility that the wrong decision may have been reached. In legal cases, it is possible for innocent defendants to be found guilty and *vice-versa*. Hypothesis tests may also reach the wrong conclusion, such as rejecting the null hypothesis when it is true (Type I error) or failing to reject the null hypothesis when it is false (Type II error).

While one may not know the value of a sample statistic before the sample is taken, it is possible to describe the range of possible values by the distribution of the random variable. The shape of the distribution is critical to conducting hypothesis tests because it allows the analyst to calculate the probability that the null hypothesis is true and the sample is not representative of the population. The normal distribution is an example of a commonly-used distribution in hypothesis testing. The normal distribution is a bell-shaped, symmetrical distribution as shown in Figure 2. As this probability becomes smaller, the evidence becomes stronger that the null hypothesis is incorrect. The analyst will select a predetermined probability level for his or her hypothesis test, and when the estimated probability falls below this level, the analyst will reject the null hypothesis.

Figure 2
Hypothetical Example of Normal Distribution for IQ of Students
(mean = 110, standard deviation = 20)

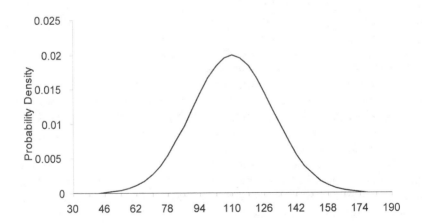

Before proceeding, some discussion is warranted regarding the advantages and disadvantages of sampling from a population. Quantitative researchers argue that relying on a subset of observations from a population can result in substantial savings in terms of time and cost. However, this introduces the possibility that the sampled items may not be representative of the population, and thus the sample statistic may not be a good estimate of the population parameter. This holds regardless of the care that is taken to ensure that all items in the population have an equal chance of being selected for the sample. In some institutional research applications, the analyst will have access to all of the data for a given population (such as the SAT scores for all freshmen), and thus would obviously want to use all of these data rather than draw a sample from the group. In these instances, statistical analyses can still be valuable depending on the way in which the results are interpreted and how the data are to be analyzed. When there are missing data for the variable of interest, the data collected from all items could still be considered a sample from a larger population. Also, by expanding the definition of "population," one can still apply traditional hypothesis tests to data on all items in a given group. Returning to the SAT example, the average SAT of freshmen in a given year may be viewed as a sample from the larger population of all freshmen over a longer period of time. Finally, when examining bivariate and multivariate relationships between variables, the concept of hypothesis testing is still useful for determining if the relationships observed in the "population" are due to random chance or are strong evidence that such a relationship exists.

Types of Quantitative Analyses

The choice of what procedure to use in a given situation is not trivial. There are literally hundreds of alternative statistical techniques that can be used in quantitative studies. Each academic discipline seems to have its own set of preferred statistical procedures that it uses, and the same procedure may have different names across disciplines. The choice of procedure can also be influenced by the size of the sample and amount of information that can be analyzed. It would be impossible to review in this chapter all of the different approaches that one might take in a quantitative research study. Rather, I will attempt to describe the types of quantitative studies that are most often performed by institutional researchers. In this chapter, I will focus exclusively on what are referred to as parametric methods for statistical analyses. These approaches are best described as those that aim to conduct hypothesis tests about an unknown population parameter, such as the average family income of all college freshmen or the linear relationship between years of experience and salary for a population of faculty. Parametric approaches are usually applied in situations where the sample sizes are sufficiently large so that reliable conclusions can be drawn about the population parameter in question without having to rely on overly restrictive assumptions. In contrast, nonparametric statistical methods are most often used when the analyst has relatively small sample sizes and is not directly interested in estimating a specific population parameter. These nonparametric approaches can be equally valuable in institutional research settings, especially when examining time-series data or institutional comparisons that often involve small amounts of information.

Quantitative studies can generally be grouped according to whether they are descriptive, bivariate, or multivariate in nature. Descriptive studies (also referred to as univariate) seek to examine one factor at a time. The goal of a descriptive study might be to test conjectures about the measure of central tendency or dispersion of a factor. For example, an institutional researcher might be interested in whether the average time-to-degree for a typical student at her institution is greater than the six-year window most often used for computing graduation rates. In contrast, bivariate studies focus on the relationship between two factors. The objective in these studies is to determine if there is some connection between two factors of interest. Returning to the previous example, an illustration of a bivariate study in institutional research would be if an analyst wanted to determine if the time-to-degree for female students is less than for male students. Finally, in a multivariate analysis, the analyst is interested is examining the relationships between multiple (more than two) variables. Using the time-to-degree example, a multivariate analysis might posit that the time-to-degree is affected by a student's gender, major, academic ability, and ability to pay for college. I will now provide more details on these general approaches.

Descriptive or Univariate Studies

Descriptive studies focus attention on the characteristics of a single factor. The most common analytical method here is to perform a hypothesis test for the value of the mean for a specific variable in the population (denoted μ). The analyst specifies a null and alternative hypothesis about the mean for the variable in the population, draws a sample of observations from the population, and calculates the mean for the sample (denoted $\bar{x}$). The student t-distribution is used as the test statistic for the hypothesis test:

$$t = \frac{\bar{x} - \mu}{s/\sqrt{n}} \tag{1}$$

where s = standard deviation of the items in the sample, n = number of observations in the sample, and $s/\sqrt{n}$ = estimated standard error for the random variable $\bar{x}$. The value for t in Equation 1 represents the distance between the sample and (hypothesized) population mean in terms of standard errors. As this distance becomes greater, the evidence becomes stronger that the null hypothesis is false.

To illustrate, suppose that an institutional researcher at a large university would like to test her belief that faculty at her institution have published an average of three journal articles in the past two years. Because it would be too expensive and time consuming to collect this information from every faculty member, she randomly surveys 64 faculty and finds that the average number of articles that they published in the last two years was 3.75 and the standard deviation was 2.0. Armed with this information, she could conduct a test of her hypothesis. The null hypothesis based on her belief is that $\mu = 3$. From the sample, she knows that $\bar{x} = 3.75$, $s = 2.0$, and $n = 64$. Accordingly, the calculated value of the test statistic is:

$$t = \frac{3.75 - 3.0}{2/\sqrt{64}} = 3.00 \tag{2}$$

This means that the sample mean of 3.75 is three standard errors above the assumed population mean of 3.0. The probability of this occurring if in fact $\mu = 3$ is only 0.13%, so the analyst would feel confident in rejecting the null hypothesis and concluding that the average number of journal articles published by faculty in the last two years is not equal to three.

Bivariate Studies

In a bivariate study, the analyst is not focused on an unknown parameter for a single variable, but rather a parameter that describes the relationship between two variables. The two most commonly used statistical tests in this category would be (a) tests of the difference between population means, and (b) correlations and simple regression analysis between two factors. In the first test, the analyst may be interested in knowing whether the population means for a given variable are the same for two different groups (denoted by subscripts 1 and 2). This is a useful approach when the grouping variable has only two possible values. An example of this might be whether the average GPA for students differs by gender. The analyst typically begins by assuming that there is no difference in the means for the two groups (i.e., $\mu_1 - \mu_2 = 0$). The student t-distribution is the appropriate test statistic in this instance, and takes the following form:

$$t = \frac{(\bar{x}_1 - \bar{x}_2) - (\mu_1 - \mu_2)}{\sqrt{\left(\frac{(n_1 - 1)s_1^2 + (n_2 - 1)s_2^2}{n_1 + n_2 - 2}\right)\left(\frac{1}{n_1} + \frac{1}{n_2}\right)}} \tag{3}$$

In this test, the random variable $(\bar{x}_1 - \bar{x}_2)$ is used to estimate the unknown population parameter $(\mu_1 - \mu_2)$, and the quantity shown in the denominator of Equation 3 is the estimated standard error of this random variable.

To illustrate, suppose that an institutional researcher would like to determine if there is a difference in the average earnings of male and female college graduates five years after graduation. The analyst surveys random samples of 100 male and 100 female college graduates and obtains the information found in Table 2.

Table 2
Information from Surveys of Randomly Selected Male and Female

Graduates

Statistic	Sample of Male Students (group 1)	Sample of Female Students (group 2)
Average earnings ($\bar{x}$)	$33,000	$32,000
Standard deviation of earnings (s)	$10,000	$ 6,000
Number of students in each sample (n)	100	100

The value of the test statistic in this case becomes:

$$t = \frac{(33,000 - 32,000) - 0}{\sqrt{\left(\frac{(100-1)(10,000^2) + (100-1)(6,000^2)}{100+100-2}\right)\left(\frac{1}{100} + \frac{1}{100}\right)}} = +0.86 \tag{4}$$

From this information, one can see that the difference in sample means is less than one standard error away from the assumed value of the population parameter. The t-distribution can be used to determine that there is a 19.49% chance of observing a difference in average salaries of $1,000 or more in samples of these sizes when in fact there is no difference in average salaries for the two respective populations. Therefore, this is not very strong evidence that the null hypothesis is false, and thus the analyst would not be able to reject the null hypothesis. Note that the analyst is not concluding that there is no difference in the two populations, but rather there is not enough evidence to safely overturn the null hypothesis.

When the grouping variable has more than two categories, the means for the categories can be compared to each other using an analysis of variance (ANOVA) approach. For example, an institutional researcher might want to know if average faculty salaries differ by academic discipline. In this instance, the null hypothesis is that the means are equal across all k groups ($\mu_1 = \mu_2 = \mu_3 = \ldots = \mu_k$). A sample is then drawn from the population and the means for each category are calculated. The *F*-distribution is used to measure the distance between these means. When all of the means are equal, $F = 0$, and as the distance between the means increases, the *F*-ratio will also increase. The hypothesis test would then reject the null hypothesis of equality of means when the *F*-ratio exceeds a predetermined threshold.

Another way of looking for whether two variables are related to one another is through the use of correlations and simple (two variable) regression analysis. Here, the analyst seeks to determine whether two variables tend to move in the same or the opposite direction. This approach is typically preferred to the two-sample *t*-test discussed earlier when the two factors of interest are continuous variables and not dichotomous, as in the case of gender. Figure 3 provides a graphical representation of a positive and negative correlation between two variables:

When there is a positive correlation between two variables, such as college GPA and high school SAT score, then higher values of one variable are associated with higher values of the other variable and *vice-versa*. In

Figure 3
Depiction of Positive and Negative Correlations

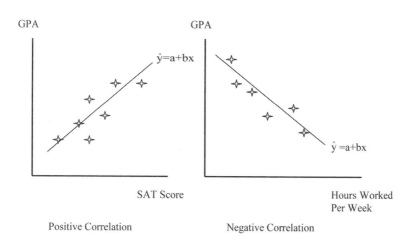

Positive Correlation   Negative Correlation

contrast, negatively correlated variables such as college GPA and average hours spent working for pay are such that higher values of one variable are associated with smaller values of the other variable.

The correlation coefficient (denoted ρ for a population and *r* for a sample) is typically used to measure the strength of the degree to which two variables move in the same or opposite direction. The sample correlation coefficient between two variables *x* and *y* is calculated as follows:

$$r = \frac{\sum (x_i - \bar{x})(y_i - \bar{y})/(n-1)}{s_x s_y} \tag{5}$$

where $\bar{x}, \bar{y}$ = means for variables x and y, respectively. The numerator of Equation 5 represents the covariance between x and y, and the denominator is the product of the standard deviations for the two variables. The correlation coefficient is restricted to fall within the range of $r = -1.00$ (perfect negative correlation) to $r = +1.00$ (perfect positive correlation). When $r = 0$, there is no correlation or linear relationship between the two variables. The analyst may conduct a hypothesis test to determine if the correlation coefficient in the sample is sufficiently large so that one can reject the null hypothesis that there is no correlation between the two variables for the larger population (i.e., $\rho = 0$).

When the analyst feels reasonably confident that he or she can identify the direction of causation between two variables, a linear regression model can also be used to measure the strength of the relationship between the variables. A regression model strives to identify the best straight line that describes how an independent variable (x) affects a dependent variable (y). The model is typically written as follows for the population in question:

$$y = \alpha + \beta x + u \tag{6}$$

where α = y-intercept of the line, β = slope of the line, and μ = random error term. As in previous examples, the true value of β is unknown because it would usually be too expensive and time consuming to obtain data on all values for x and y in the population and compute the slope of the corresponding regression line. Therefore, a quantitative researcher would draw a sample of observations for x and y and then estimate the linear relationship between them in the sample. The sample regression line is then expressed as follows:

$$\hat{y} = a + bx \tag{7}$$

where $\hat{y}$ = predicted value of y in the sample, a = estimated y-intercept from the sample, and b = estimated slope from the sample. Graphical depictions of these lines are shown in Figure 3. The slope from the sample is estimated as follows:

$$b = \frac{\sum (x_i - \bar{x})(y_i - \bar{y})/(n-1)}{s_x^2} \tag{8}$$

which can be interpreted as the covariance between x and y divided by the variance for x. The y-intercept is then computed as $a = \bar{y} - b\bar{x}$.

The regression equation has several uses in institutional research applications. First, the model can be used to test hypotheses about the relationship between two variables in the population. An analyst may have a belief or hypothesis about the value of the population slope that he or she wants to test. Typically, the null hypothesis is that the variable x has no linear effect on y ($\beta = 0$). A test of this form is often referred to as a significance test, because rejection of the null hypothesis leads to the conclusion that x has an effect on y. A sample of observations on x and y is drawn and the slope in the sample is calculated as shown in Equation 8. The sample slope (b) can then be used as evidence to evaluate the null hypothesis as follows:

$$t = \frac{b - \beta}{s_b} \tag{9}$$

where s_b = standard error of b. The calculated t-ratio is then used in the same way as the calculated t-ratios in previous examples to conduct the hypothesis test. The regression model can also be used to obtain predictions of y (denoted $\hat{y}$) given values for x. Once the slope and intercept are calculated for the sample line, the analyst can substitute values for x into the equation and determine the predicted value for y.

To illustrate both uses of regression analysis, suppose that an institutional researcher would like to determine if there is a relationship between a student's high school rank and academic performance in college. Due to the timing of the variables, the analyst sets high school rank as the independent variable (x) and college GPA as the dependent variable (y). He obtains data on a random sample of 500 students and finds that the slope and intercept are 0.10 and 1.50 respectively. The regression line is then written as:

$$= 1.50 + 0.01x \tag{10}$$

To test the null hypothesis that there is no linear relationship between high school rank and college GPA in the population ($b = 0$), she would then calculate the t-ratio from Equation 9. Assuming that the standard error of b is 0.002, the calculated t-ratio is $0.01 / 0.002 = +5.00$. Because there is very little chance of obtaining a slope of $+0.01$ or greater when $b = 0$, this is strong evidence that $b \neq 0$ and thus the null hypothesis can be rejected. The analyst could also use this equation to predict a student's college GPA based on the student's high school rank. For example, a student with a high

high school rank of 70% would have a predicted college GPA of $\hat{y} = 1.50 + 0.01(70) = 2.20$.

A few words of caution are warranted at this point with regard to what can and cannot be concluded from a regression analysis such as this. As noted earlier, in order to perform a regression analysis, the analyst must specify the direction of causation between two variables. There are several ways in which this might be done. An analyst may rely on a particular education theory that argues that a given variable x affects another variable y. For example, human capital theory suggests that a person's wages in the labor market is affected by his or her skills that contribute to a person's productivity. Therefore, institutional researchers who conduct salary equity studies often posit that a faculty member's educational attainment or years of experience would possibly affect the faculty member's salary. A second way in which decisions about causality may be made is by appealing to the timing of the two variables in question. To illustrate, an analyst who is studying the retention of college students may construct a model where the student's high school GPA has a causal effect on whether or not the student returns to college for their sophomore year. The direction of causation here may be justified by the analysts because a student's high school GPA was by definition determined prior to the student's decision about returning to the institution.

In either instance, the researcher needs to recognize that any conclusions drawn about causality are conditional on the initial decision made about causality. This is important for several reasons. First, the theories used to determine causality may be incorrect. Second, in some situations the direction of causality may be ambiguous. This could arise when competing theories offer alternative hypotheses about causality between variables of interest, or when the timing of the variables is such that the direction of causality is unclear. If an analyst posits that a particular variable x affects y, when in fact the relationship is the other way around, and the t-ratio shown in Equation 9 is statistically insignificant, the analyst would conclude that x affects y when the analyst should have concluded that y affects x. Finally, in all of these instances it should be recognized that even when one concludes that β is nonzero, the analyst has not proven that the variable x causes y to change. The significant relationship between two variables could in reality reflect another relationship that is not observed by the analyst. For example, suppose that a regression study of college attendance found that high school students who come from families with college-educated parents are more likely than other high school students to attend college. This does not necessarily mean that higher parental education per se influenced a student's decision to attend college. It could be that parental education is associated with other factors such as the emphasis that parents place on their children's education, the amount of time that parents can spend with their children in support of their education, and so on, which really have the causal impact on college attendance. Accordingly, parental education may be a placeholder for other factors that truly have a causal impact on college attendance. While it is still commonplace for analysts to use causal language when describing their findings, these caveats should be kept in mind.

Multivariate Studies

Finally, there are many instances in institutional research where a multivariate analysis is desirable. In most situations, there are likely to be multiple independent factors that could have an effect on a given dependent variable. A student's college GPA is likely to be affected not only by his/her high school rank, but also the student's gender, SAT score, hours spent studying per week, academic major, and so on. The same argument would hold for virtually any dependent variable of interest to institutional researchers.

The most commonly used multivariate statistical procedure for institutional research purposes is referred to as multiple regression analysis. The linear equation describing the dependent variable needs to be expanded to include all of the k measurable factors that are thought to influence y:

$$y = \alpha + \beta_1 x_1 + \beta_2 x_2 + ... + \beta_k x_k + u \qquad (11)$$

The estimated coefficients are interpreted as partial effects, meaning how a one-unit change in a given x will affect y holding all of the other x variables constant. The analyst can then use this model to test hypotheses about the population slope for each variable (β_k) in the same way as before, and can obtain predicted values for y after substituting values for all x variables into the equation.

Suppose that an institutional researcher wants to understand why the six-year graduation rate for universities (y) fluctuates across institutions. She uses educational theories and logic about the timing of variables to posit that an institution's graduation rate may be affected by the average SAT score of freshmen (x_1), the enrollment level of the university (x_2), the percentage of freshmen who live off-campus (x_3), and/or whether the institution is public (x_4). Note that because the fourth variable is qualitative in nature, it must be converted into a numerical variable for inclusion in the regression model. In this instance, the analyst created a dummy variable x_4 = 1 if the institution is public and x_4 = 0 otherwise. She obtains data for a random sample of 200 institutions (See Table 3). The coefficient for the first variable indicates that, holding an institution's enrollment level, percentage of freshmen living off-campus, and public/private status constant, a one point increase in the average SAT score of freshmen would lead to a predicted 0.02 percent increase in the university's graduation rate. If the estimated y-intercept is 40, then the linear equation would be written as

Table 3
Results from a Random Sample of 200 Institutions

Statistics	Independent Variables			
	Average SAT score of freshmen (x_1)	Enrollment level of the university (x_2)	Percentage of freshmen who live off-campus (x_3)	Whether institution is public or private (x_4)
Slope (b)	0.020	0.003	-0.100	-0.005
Standard error (s_b)	0.006	0.005	0.016	0.010
Calculated t-ratio	+3.33	+0.60	-6.25	-0.50

follows:

$$\hat{y} = 40 + 0.02x_1 + 0.003x_2 - 0.100x_k - 0.005x_4 \qquad (12)$$

Four separate hypothesis tests can now be conducted to determine if any of the four factors have a significant effect on an institution's graduation rate. The null hypotheses would be that each factor has no effect on an institution's graduation rate ($\beta_1 = 0$, $\beta_2 = 0$, $\beta_3 = 0$, $\beta_4 = 0$). Based on the calculated t-ratios shown above, the analyst would reject the null hypothesis for the first and third variables and conclude that the average SAT score of freshmen and the percentage of freshmen who live off campus each have an effect on a university's graduation rate. In contrast, there is not enough evidence for the analyst to conclude that either the size or the public/private status of the institution have an effect on the graduation rate, holding the other two variables constant. The analyst should also recognize that the significant findings between the first and third variables and graduation rates has not proven that there are causal relationships between these specific factors. For example, it may not be that the average SAT score of freshmen per se has a causal effect on an institution's graduation rate, but rather factors such as student aptitude or test-taking ability have the true causal impacts on graduation rates. It is the correlation between SAT scores and student aptitude and test-taking ability that gives rise to the statistical conclusion that SAT scores have a significant effect on an institution's graduation rate.

Concluding Thoughts

In this chapter, I have attempted to outline the general approach that quantitatively oriented institutional researchers use in their work. Quantitative analyses are based on the notion of using the results from a sample for a given population to say something about what the results would have been had the entire population been examined. Analysts use probability statements to determine the likelihood of observing the results obtained in a given sample if the null hypothesis was true and repeated samples were drawn from the population. As this likelihood decreases, the fact that the results were obtained for the sample in hand becomes stronger evidence that the null hypothesis is incorrect.

This approach is grounded in what is referred to as a positivist philosophy towards research issues where the analyst believes that his or her job is to try and uncover evidence about the causal relationship between factors of interest. As noted in the introduction, there are alternative epistemological schools of thought on this issue that are not explored here. Even within the positivist philosophy, one may advocate for using either a quantitative or qualitative approach to research. Carol Trosset's chapter in this volume explores in detail how institutional researchers may use qualitative methods to explore issues of interest.

Education researchers often debate the relative merits of quantitative and qualitative methods and end up firmly entrenched in one empirical "camp" or the other. I would like to propose an alternative view, however, that institutional researchers should consider the situations under which each of these empirical approaches may yield useful information. If done correctly, the two approaches to inquiry can complement each other and result in a more complete analysis of the issue at hand.

Quantitative methods have the advantage of being able to generalize findings to larger populations of interest, and yet have been criticized because they must rely on constructs that are measurable and available to the analyst. In the earlier example that I used of the impact of parental education on a student's postsecondary attendance, the quantitative researcher would be limited in his or her ability to uncover the more difficult to measure family attributes that may, in fact, have a causal relationship with student aspirations. While qualitative studies generally are not designed to apply their findings to larger populations, their advantage over quantitative studies is that through data collection methods such as in-depth interviews, they can explore more subtle aspects of a problem than would usually be possible in a quantitative study.

Viewed in this way, it can be seen that quantitative and qualitative methodologies complement each other and thus could be used together in many educational settings to enrich our analyses of education issues. To illustrate how this might be done, I previously conducted a quantitative study in New Hampshire of how socioeconomic factors of a community affected the percentages of public high school 10th graders who successfully passed the state's standardized test (Toutkoushian & Curtis, 2005). A school's pass rate on the standardized test had been used as one measure of the quality of the school. The analysis showed that approximately half of the variations across public high schools in their pass rates could be explained by these socioeconomic factors. After reading the study, several officials across the state inquired as to what factors explained the remaining 50% of the variation in pass rates across schools. I informed them that the quantitative methods used here could not adequately address these issues. The quantitative approach provided some answers to policymakers, but left others to be explored. The state's Department of Education subsequently conducted a qualitative study of those high schools that the quantitative study had revealed had higher-than-anticipated pass rates on the standardized test. Without the quantitative analysis, the state would not have known where it would be best to conduct more in-depth interviews. While the results from the qualitative approach could not be generalized to all high schools in the state, they might lead to ideas for future quantitative studies that could test hypotheses about the findings from the qualitative study. I believe that a similar model of mixed approaches to institutional research problems can yield valuable insights into the phenomena that we seek to explain through our work.

References and Suggested Background Readings

Black, T. (1999). *Doing quantitative research in the social sciences.* Thousand Oaks, CA: Sage Publications.

Fraenkel, J., & Wallen, N. (2000). *How to design & evaluate research in education* (4th ed.). Boston: McGraw-Hill.

Gibbons, J. (1997). *Nonparametric methods for quantitative analysis* (3rd ed.). Columbus, OH: American Sciences Press.

Higgins, J. (2004). *Introduction to modern nonparametric statistics* (1st ed.). Stamford, CT: Thomson Learning.

Kenny, D. (1979). *Correlation and causality.* New York: John Wiley & Sons.

McMillan, J., & Schumacher, S. (2001). *Research in education: A conceptual introduction* (5th ed.). New York: Addison Wesley Longman.

Singleton, R., & Straits, B. (1999). *Approaches to social research* (3rd ed.). New York: Oxford University Press.

Toutkoushian, R. K., & Curtis, T. (2005). The effects of socioeconomic factors on public high school outcomes and rankings: Evidence from New Hampshire. *Journal of Educational Research*, 98, 259-271.

Chapter 4
Using a Mixed-Method Approach to Study a University Faculty and Staff Annual Giving Campaign

William E. Knight
Bowling Green University

The pragmatists argue that a false dichotomy existed between qualitative and quantitative approaches and that researchers should make the most efficient use of both paradigms in understanding social phenomena (Creswell, 1994, p. 176)

We believe that the quantitative-qualitative argument is essentially unproductive . . . quantitative and qualitative methods are "inextricably intertwined", not only at the level of specific data sets but also at the levels of study design and analysis. (Miles & Huberman, 1994, p. 41)

Unquestionably all research designs are flawed. By integrating both qualitative and quantitative research, however, the deficiencies of one approach can be offset by the advantages of another. (Creswell, Goodchild, & Turner, 1996)

Just as machines that were originally created for separate functions such as printing, faxing, and copying have now been combined into a single integrated technology unit, so too methods that were originally created as distinct, stand-alone approaches can now be combined into more sophisticated and multifunctional designs. (Patton, 2002, p. 252)

The Context of the Study

Despite an economic upturn in many areas since the turn of the Millennium, many state-assisted institutions continue to face financial hardship. Particularly in states with traditionally manufacturing-based economies, continuing resource constraints affecting state governments, hesitancy to raise taxes, and ever-increasing expenditure demands for Medicaid, K-12 education, and other priorities have led to cuts in state support for colleges and universities (American Association of State Colleges and Universities, 2006; Walters, 2006). As state support has moved from a condition of failing to keep pace with institutional expenses to actually declining, and tuition is legislatively constrained by state government, market forces, or both, campuses are forced to make hard choices. They can downsize, reallocate funds, and/or cultivate non-traditional sources of revenue.

Increasing private fund raising and externally sponsored research and service activities are key strategies for colleges and universities facing such circumstances (Brittingham & Pezullo, 1990; Rhodes, 1997; Worth, 1993). It is often difficult to build the infrastructure necessary for success in those activities, particularly at small and medium-sized institutions with a past history of limited success. In the area of private fund raising, development professionals have found that contributions from external donors are often influenced by the success of internal faculty and staff annual giving campaigns. Such internal campaigns often serve as an indicator of institutional vitality and success.

Bowling Green State University (BGSU) faces many of the issues noted above. State budget cuts coupled with constraints on fee increases have forced the issue of gaining revenue from non-traditional sources to become a priority. The campus is in the midst of a major comprehensive campaign. Both as evidence for external donors and as a fundraising strategy of its own, the University initiated an annual giving campaign, known as the Family Campaign, among faculty, administrative staff, classified staff, and retirees in 1998-1999. The first year $454,985 was raised and 35% of employees contributed. At the end of the 2001-2002 fiscal year, when the study was carried out, $699,020 was raised and the participation rate was 48%. In 2005-2006, $803,030 was raised and 54% of employees contributed. BGSU's Family Campaign has been among the most successful of its type in the country, as evidenced by its receipt of the Council for the Advancement and Support of Education (CASE) Seal of Excellence for Philanthropy Award in 2001 and given the attention it has received from other institutions.

Despite the success of the Family Campaign, its leaders remain interested in continuing to improve its results. While the Office of Development could determine that the participation rates in the Family Campaign were highest for retirees, then administrative staff members, then faculty members, and lowest for classified (hourly) staff members, more detailed information that could be used to improve marketing for the campaign was not available. For example, it would be useful to know whether participation varied significantly among staff groups (*e.g.*, among clerical vs. skilled craft vs. service/maintenance staff members), by gender and race, and by whether employees resided near the campus (suggesting differences in involvement). Also, it was recognized that faculty members, given their compensation relative to their participation levels, had the greatest untapped giving capacity, but it was not known why more faculty members didn't give, what their perceptions were about the Family Campaign, and what changes could be made that would encourage greater levels of giving.

A considerable amount of literature exists concerning fundraising, by non-profit organizations in general and by colleges and universities in particular, that offers some hints about donor motivations. People give for philanthropic reasons, to gain acclaim and friendship, to address their need to overcome guilt, in order to repay society for advantages that they have received, as an investment in activities that may later benefit them (*e.g.*, sponsoring research projects), and in order to obtain tangible perquisites such as honorary degrees (Pezzullo & Brittingham, 1993). Giving is motivated by values (Greenfield, 1999). Giving is related to marital status, gender, age, income, educational attainment, religion, tax policy, established levels of trust and involvement with the institution, perceptions of the institution's management, and the perception of fundraising activities as ethical (Brittingham & Pezullo, 1990; Pezzullo & Brittingham, 1993; Ciconte & Jacob, 2001). On a more conceptual level, theories on relationship-centered communication with constituents, such as Grunig's (2001) two-way symmetrical model, hold that research and dialogue with fundraisers can promote changes and attitudes and behaviors among donors. One study was found that addressed specifically the issue of faculty and staff participation in a college or university annual giving campaign. Holland and Miller (1999) surveyed full-time faculty at three universities to ascertain the relationship between faculty characteristics, motivations for giving, and fundraising strategies. They found that senior faculty members who were not graduates of their employing institution were more inclined to give; that primary motives for giving included altruism, a sense of social responsibility, self-fulfillment, professional attitude, conviction, and institutional loyalty; and that telephone solicitation was the most effective fundraising strategy.

Discussions with staff of the Office of Development and campaign volunteers, as well as review of the literature, suggested two research questions for a study that was carried out by BGSU's Office of Institutional Research in 2002: (a) Are there significant relationships between faculty and staff characteristics and their giving behavior?, and (b) What are the knowledge and perceptions of the Family Campaign and suggestions for improving participation rates among faculty members?

Methods
The study was one characterized by Creswell, Goodchild, and Turner (1996) as using both methods equally and in parallel. Quantitative and qualitative approaches were applied separately to the research questions so the strengths of each could be maximized (Morse, 2003). First, development, human resources, and alumni records were merged and analyzed to examine significant relationships between employee giving and personal characteristics including employee type, job classification, longevity at the University, gender, race, full-time vs. part-time status, salary, city of residence, and whether the employee was an alumnus. Decisions on what

variables to include in the data set were shaped by both the research questions and availability. Given the confidential nature of the development data, only the author was involved in the manipulation and analysis of the data and the results were shared in a summary format only with the development staff and campaign volunteers. A series of cross-tabulations, t-tests, and a logistic regression analysis were carried out to examine statistically significant patterns between various demographic characteristics and whether or not employees contributed to the 2001-2002 Family Campaign.

Second, interviews were carried out with twelve BGSU full-time faculty members. This number provided manageability, representativeness, and information richness (Kemper, Stringfield, & Teddlie, 2003). The faculty participants were selected through random stratified sampling in order to ensure that the profile of the participants was roughly equivalent to that of all full-time faculty members with respect to college, longevity at the University, gender, and Family Campaign participation. Eight interview questions were developed to gather information about faculty members' overall knowledge of the Family Campaign, best methods of receiving information, why faculty choose to give or not to give, how the Family Campaign should best be marketed to faculty, barriers or situations that prevent faculty from participating, possible concerns over the use of funds raised, the effect of giving by the academic leadership on the giving of rank and file faculty, and other information that participants cared to provide. The interview protocol (see appendix) was developed by the author and the development staff in consultation with campaign volunteers. Data analysis yielded two types of findings: detailed descriptions of each case, which were used to document uniqueness, and shared patterns that emerge across cases (Patton, 2002). Data analysis involved breaking material into small units of observation, developing initial themes or categories within the findings, and considering alternative interpretations that will either confirm the initial themes or lead to the creation of new ones. The researcher attempted to bracket his knowledge and presuppositions so as not to taint the findings (Crotty, 1998), but rather to focus on participants' perspectives (Bogdan & Biklen, 1998). A peer debriefer was used to test themes and alternative conclusions (Lincoln & Guba, 1985). Preliminary conclusions were shared with participants for their confirmation and elaboration; this constitutes a member check (Lincoln & Guba, 1985). An audit trail of study materials served to provide for dependability and confirmability.

Findings

Quantitative Phase

Table 1 provides the results of a series of univariate statistical tests. There was a statistically significant difference in the giving rate by employee

Table 1
Differences in Faculty and Staff Giving Behavior Related to
Employee Characteristics

| Employee Group | Gave to the 2001-2002 Family Campaign | | |
	No	Yes	ς^2 (df)
Employee Group 134.6*** (2)			
Administrative Staff	226 40.3%	335 59.7%	
Faculty	722 65.4%	382 34.6%	
Classified Staff	693 68.5%	318 31.5%	
Work Category Group 333.8*** (6)			
Executive/Administrative/ Managerial	27 17.8%	125 82.2%	
Other Professional	158 40.5%	232 59.5%	
Faculty	62 67.2%	306 32.8%	
Clerical-Secretarial	298 55.5%	239 44.5%	
Technical-Paraprofessional	76 62.8%	45 37.2%	
Skilled Crafts	33 89.2%	4 10.8%	
Service Maintenance	290 89.8%	33 10.2%	

Full-Time or Part-Time
211.9*** (1)

Full-Time	1305 56.0%	1024 44.0%
Part-Time	336 96.8%	11 3.2%

Race
18.5** (4)

Black	30 49.2%	31 50.8%
White	1304 59.1%	902 40.9%
American Indian	6 66.7%	3 33.3%
Hispanic	61 76.3%	19 23.8%
Asian	35 77.8%	10 22.2%

Alumnus
76.1*** (1)

No	1382 65.5%	725 34.4%
Yes	259 45.5%	310 54.5%

Live in Bowling Green
63.5*** (1)

No	938 68.7%	428 31.3%
Yes	703 53.7%	607 46.3%

Gave Previously
    699.0*** (1)

	No	Yes
No	828 88.6%	107 11.4%
Yes	486 34.4%	926 65.6%

Gender
    0.5 (1)

	No	Yes
Female	898 61.1%	571 38.9%
Male	612 59.7%	413 40.3%

	Gave to the 2001-2002 Family Campaign		
Employee Group	No	Yes	t (df)

	No	Yes
Mean Total Previous Giving 8.6*** (2347)	$260	$1,477
Median 2001-2002 Salary 13.1*** (2312)	$35,804	$45,004
Mean Years Employed at BGSU 7.5*** (2674)	10.6	13.4

* p < .05   ** p < .01   *** p < .001

group, with administrative staff more likely to give than faculty or classified staff members. More details can be understood when the employee groups are further subdivided by more specific work categories. This analysis also showed a statistically significant difference, with employees in the Executive/Administrative/Managerial and Other Professional groups (both administrative staff) most likely to give and employees in the Skilled Crafts and Service Maintenance categories (both classified staff) least likely to give. Full-time employees were significantly more likely to give. Blacks and Whites were significantly more likely to give than Asians or Hispanics; the giving rate for American Indians fell in between these groups. It should be noted that the small number of persons in the minority groups tends to inflate the percentages. Employees who were alumni were significantly more likely to give. Employee home zip codes were used to determine whether or not employees lived in the City of Bowling Green. Those employees who lived in Bowling Green were more significantly likely to give. There was a statistically significant difference in Family Campaign 2001-2002 giving rates based upon whether employees had ever given previously to the University; those who gave previously were much more likely to contribute again in 2001-2002. Although males were slightly more likely to give than females, the difference was *not* statistically significant. Employees with higher previous giving totals were significantly more likely to give in 2001-2002. Those with higher salaries were significantly more likely to give. There was a statistically significant difference in giving rates based upon the number of years employees had worked at BGSU; those employed for more years were more likely to give.

A logistic regression analysis was used to determine the relative strengths of the various employee demographic characteristics in explaining or predicting employee giving behavior. These results (shown in Table 2 for statistically significant effects only) reveal that having a previous giving history is by far the strongest positive predictor of giving to the Family Campaign. Other predictors include (in order), not being in the Faculty or Service-Maintenance work categories, being White, living in Bowling Green, having a higher salary, and not being in the Technical-Paraprofessional or Skilled Crafts work categories. Race was recoded into minority vs. White for the regression analysis; the fact that being a minority was associated with not giving to the Family Campaign can be reconciled with the results of the earlier analyses due to the fact that the plurality of minority employees at BGSU are Hispanic and this group was among the least likely to give.

Qualitative Phase

All of the interview participants could articulate a basic sense of the purpose of the Family Campaign as a method for faculty to include BGSU in their charitable giving, to contribute to the University's revenue base, and to enhance BGSU's mission. A few participants noted that faculty-staff giving is used for external relations purposes to leverage gifts. With one or two exceptions, faculty participants had only a general sense that contributions to a variety of University funds "count" for the Family Campaign; one or two persons specifically stated that they were aware that contributions to sources such as the athletic club or the public television station "count." With one exception, none seemed to be aware of the existence of detailed fund lists to which contributions can be directed. The one exception was a faculty member in the College of Technology, who noted that a booklet of giving opportunities specific to that college was developed and widely circulated.

Table 2
Results of Logistic Regression Analysis Concerning
Faculty and Staff Giving

Predictor Exp (B)	B	SE	Wald
Previous Giving History 12.90	2.56	0.14	324.38**
Work Category: Faculty 0.31	-1.19	0.26	21.16**
Work Category: Service- Maintenance 0.21	-1.58	0.41	14.86**
Race (Minority) 0.54	-0.62	0.20	9.31**
Live in Bowling Green 1.40	0.33	0.11	8.57**
Salary 1.00	0.00	0.00	8.06**
Work Category: Technical- Paraprofessional 0.38	-0.97	0.37	6.84**
Work Category: Skilled Crafts 0.17	-1.79	0.69	6.66**

** $p < .01$

Many participants noted that they were unsure how the funds were used. Frustration was also expressed over the situation where faculty (or spouses) were also alumni and felt pressured by the University to give to both alumni fundraising efforts as well as the Family Campaign; participants felt that the Office of Development could be doing a more effective job of not making multiple "asks."

Most faculty members agreed that the current practice of using departmental representatives as the primary sources of information about the Family Campaign is a good one. Two participants stated that use of departmental representatives was perceived as too much of a "hard sell" and that they would prefer receiving written notices through methods such as direct mail, notices placed into pay stubs, and information in the faculty-staff newsletter. Receiving e-mail and hearing multiple verbal reminders in various meeting and University events were noted as effective communication methods by one person. Most noted that faculty are so inundated with communications that no one way of providing information about the Family Campaign is particularly effective. The faculty member in the College of Technology stated that sending lists of college- or department-specific giving opportunities to faculty in each area would be effective. Others agreed that printed materials in general were effective.

A wide range of responses was generated to the question of why some faculty members choose to contribute and others do not. Several senior faculty members cited poor morale and lack of community spirit or lack of faculty bonding with the University in general. Some participants noted that they choose to participate because they do have a strong allegiance and feel connected to the University. It was noted by more than one participant that faculty have the greatest allegiance to their departments, then to their colleges, and finally to the University in general; as long as the Family Campaign is marketed (or perceived to be marketed) to general University-wide issues rather than department-specific needs, faculty participation will be limited. In related comments, other participants noted that they pay for instructional materials out of their own pockets due to inadequate departmental operating budgets, and therefore they are hard pressed to give even more. These participants agree that direct appeals to support needs at the individual department level might cause more faculty to participate. Some participants stated that they declined to participate (or stopped participating) due to disagreements with Family Campaign priorities (or perceived priorities). Another participant noted that he chooses not to participate because of a fundamental philosophical disagreement with the idea of asking the employees of an organization to give money to their employer. He stated that faculty members make contributions to students every day while being employed at a far lower rate of compensation than could be had in the private sector. One participant noted that since many faculty members are unsure of how their contributions will be used and also because they can only contribute small amounts, they fail to contribute at all.

A recurring theme among most of the faculty participants was that the Family Campaign's marketing approach of noting the variety of giving targets available to donors and highlighting a few University-wide giving targets is not succeeding with faculty because they want to see very specific ideas of how their contributions will benefit their own departments. Providing department-specific listings of giving opportunities and showing tailored examples of how this giving has benefited (or could benefit) each department would be a much more effective approach with many faculty. Sharing more detailed information after each year's Family Campaign about how the contributions were actually used was also noted as a useful approach. Student scholarships and faculty research and travel support were noted as particularly appealing giving targets for faculty. Any perceived connection between the Family Campaign and athletics seemed to be a negative for many participants. It is particularly important among faculty that the Family Campaign not be perceived as a "hard sell."

Several participants stated that the low salaries of BGSU faculty members compared to those at other universities prevent greater participation in the Family Campaign. Newer faculty who are earlier in their careers and not tenured are often starting families, paying off student loans, and personally supplementing their own research and travel expenses, memberships in professional associations, etc. at the same time that their pay is the lowest, and their affiliation is perhaps the least as compared with other faculty; these conditions make it difficult for newer faculty to contribute. Conversely, many of the University's most senior faculty are saving for retirement. It was often noted that faculty are asked to contribute to many causes within their communities, to the institutions from which they graduated, etc. As noted above and discussed further below, uncertainty about how their contributions will be used may represent a barrier to participation for some faculty.

Participants were asked whether concern over fund usage prevented some faculty from participating in the Family Campaign. Several were unsure, and some were unconcerned about this issue. Several noted that they are not concerned about diversion of funds from specified targets but rather about being able to specify the source of their contributions as specifically as they would like. For example, some would like to donate to specific areas not already established, but they are unable to themselves meet the minimum dollar thresholds necessary to establish new funds. It was suggested that staff of the Office of Development meet with each department to explore faculty interests in pooling monies to establish new funds. Again, it was suggested that detailed information be shared each year after the Family Campaign concludes about how funds were used.

Most of the participants stated that they did not know about the giving behavior of leaders of their departments and colleges, although many expected that academic leaders should give. Most said that they would not be influenced by this even if they knew whether their department or college leaders gave.

Impact of the Study

Prior to providing implications for the study it is necessary to acknowledge its limitations. The study was carried out at a single institution at a single point in time. While the dozen full-time faculty members interviewed were proportionately representative of all BGSU full-time faculty with respect to gender college, longevity, and participation in the 2001-2002 Family Campaign, there is no way to ensure that their perceptions were truly representative of all full-time faculty. Because the goal of the interviews was to learn more about perceptions of the Family Campaign specifically on the part of full-time faculty, their responses cannot be generalized to any other employee groups. The nature of the Family Campaign at BGSU and how faculty and staff react to it may be different than at other institutions.

Given the findings of the quantitative portion of the study, it was suggested that development staff and volunteers may also wish to consider the usefulness of solicitation of part-time employees and perhaps to limit their solicitation (part-time staff members are no longer solicited). It was also suggested that they may also wish to very carefully contact selected faculty and staff members of American Indian, Asian, and Hispanic heritage and further explore perceptions of and participation in efforts such as the Family Campaign (this was done). Third, it was suggested that Alumni and Development may wish to combine and carefully consider their efforts concerning solicitation of employees who are also university alumni since these persons are more likely to contribute, but they are also sometimes frustrated by multiple solicitations; careful attention to this issue may lead to positive results (this remains a challenge). Fourth, since employees who do not live in the city where the university's main campus is located are significantly less likely to contribute, it may be useful to explore methods of making these people feel more integrated with the university community (this has not been addressed).

Because of the fact that those employees who contributed to the Family Campaign previously are much more likely to do so again, the importance of donor recognition cannot be over-emphasized (this remains a key part of the Family Campaign). While the strong relationship between salary and giving behavior is understandable, it may be appropriate to stress, especially to faculty and classified staff groups, more strongly that participation, not the dollar amount of contributions, is the goal at BGSU (we continue to communicate this). While the finding is taken as positive that participation increases with longevity at the university, these results suggest that more proactive outreach about the Family Campaign and like efforts may need to be done with new employee groups (this has happened).

The findings of the qualitative phase of the study suggested that the development staff would be well served to change, target, and expand its efforts with faculty members concerning programs like the Family Campaign. While some faculty members have strong feelings about the appropriateness of employee annual giving programs and others have a negative feeling about the University that relates to lack of participation, the interviews suggested that many faculty might choose to participate if they better understood the purposes of the Family Campaign and the use of funds collected. This is especially true if they could see the relationship between participation in the Family Campaign and the addressing of needs and priorities in their individual departments. While clearly requiring considerable time and effort personalizing the Family Campaign to faculty—not only as a unique employee group but to different sets of faculty in different areas of the university—may lead to substantially improved results. Implementing these findings remains an ongoing effort.

Lessons Learned Concerning Methods

While some (*e.g.*, Guba & Lincoln, 1988) have argued that the underlying epistemology of the quantitative and qualitative paradigms suggests that never the twain shall meet, others such as Patton (2002, p. 252) hold that the "practical mandate in evaluation to gather the most relevant possible information for evaluation users outweighs concerns about methodological purity based on epistemological and philosophical arguments." This was the case for the study described in this chapter.

Tashakkori and Teddlie (2003, p. 674) propose three ways in which mixed methods may be superior to single approach designs:

1. Mixed methods research can answer research questions that other methodologies cannot.
2. Mixed methods research provides better (stronger) inferences.
3. Mixed methods provide the opportunity for presenting a greater diversity of divergent views.

The authors suggest that mixed method approaches allow theory confirmation (through quantitative techniques) and exploration (possibly leading to theory generation, through qualitative techniques) to take place simultaneously. This was certainly the case with the BGSU study, as it provided for findings of previous studies as well as ideas from Family Campaign staff and volunteers to be confirmed/refuted at the same time that faculty members' perceptions were explored. The study provided stronger and more useful results than could have been obtained through either method alone. Finally, it made it possible for both patterns among group members as well as individual differences to be articulated.

Appendix: Faculty Interview Protocol

Before Beginning Each Interview:

- Introductions
- Remind participants of the purpose of the study.
- Participants have the right not to respond to any question.
- All materials will be kept confidential and pseudonyms will be used in reporting out the responses.
- There are no right or wrong answers.
- Ask permission to tape.

1. Can you briefly describe what you know about the BGSU Family Campaign? [probes: Purpose? What contributions "count?" Where can gifts be directed?]
2. What methods of hearing about the Family Campaign are most effective? [probes: Departmental reps.? Printed materials? Other?]

3. What are some reasons that you think faculty either give or do not give? [probes: institutional loyalty, professional attitude, social responsibility vs. conviction, self-fulfillment]
4. What are the reasons for giving by faculty to which the Development Office should appeal?
5. What are some of the situations or barriers that prevent faculty from contributing? [probe: Already contributing to other organizations?]
6. Do you think faculty are satisfied with their sense that their contributions are being used in the ways that were intended? [probe: Is more acknowledgement needed of receipt of gifts directed towards a particular area?]
7. Does the giving behavior of those in a leadership role in department make a difference in the giving behavior of all faculty in that department?
8. Are we asking the right questions? What else would you like to tell us about the Family Campaign?

At the End of Each Interview:

Thank you.
Promise to share results as a member check.

References

American Association of State Colleges and Universities. (2006, January). 2006 Shaping up as a "keeping up" year in the States. *Policy Matters, 3*. Retrieved July 9, 2006 from http://www.aascu.org/policy_matters/ v3_1/default.htm (active as of 2/6/07)

Bogdan, R. C., & Biklen, S. K. (1998). *Qualitative research in education: An introduction to theory and methods*. Boston: Allyn & Bacon.

Brittingham, B. E., & Pezullo, T. R. (1990). *The campus green: Fund raising in higher education*. Washington, DC: School of Education and Human Development, the George Washington University.

Ciconte, B. L., & Jacob, J. G. (2001). *Fundraising basics: A complete guide* (2nd ed.). Gaithersburg, MD: Aspen Publishers.

Creswell, J. W. (1994). *Research design: Qualitative and quantitative approaches*. Thousand Oaks, CA: Sage Publications.

Creswell, J. W., Goodchild, L. F., & Turner, P. P. (1996). Integrated qualitative and quantitative research: Epistemology, history, and designs. In J. C. Smart (Ed.), *Higher education: Handbook of theory and research, Vol. XI*. (pp. 90-136). New York: Agathon Press.

Crotty, M. (1998). *The foundations of social research: Meaning and perspective in the research process*. Thousand Oaks, CA: Sage Publications.

Greenfield, J. M. (1999). *Fundraising: Evaluating and managing the fund development process* (2nd ed.). New York: Wiley.

Grunig, J. E. (2001). Two-way symmetrical public relations: Past, present, and future. In R. L. Heath (Ed.), *Handbook of public relations* (pp. 11-30). Thousand Oaks, CA: Sage Publications.

Guba, E. G., & Lincoln, Y. S. (1988). Do inquiry paradigms imply inquiry methodologies? In D. Fetterman (Ed.), *Qualitative approaches to evaluation in education: The silent scientific revolution* (pp. 89-115). New York: Praeger.

Holland, A. P., & Miller, M. T. (1999). *Faculty as donors: Why they give to their employing institutions.* ERIC Document Reproduction Service No. ED439648.

Kemper, E. A., Stringfield, S., & Teddlie, C. (2003). Mixed methods sampling strategies in social science research. In A. Tashakkori and C. Teddlie (Eds.), *Handbook of mixed methods in social and behavioral research* (pp. 273-296). Thousand Oaks, CA: Sage Publications.

Lincoln, Y. S., & Guba, E. G. (1985). *Naturalistic inquiry.* Beverly Hills, CA: Sage Publications.

Miles, M. B., & Huberman, A. M. (1994). *Qualitative data analysis.* (2nd ed.). Thousand Oaks, CA: Sage Publications.

Morse, J. M. (2003). Principles of mixed methods and multimethod research design. In A. Tashakkori and C. Teddlie (Eds.), *Handbook of mixed methods in social and behavioral research* (pp. 189-208). Thousand Oaks, CA: Sage Publications.

Patton, M. Q. (2002). *Qualitative research & evaluation methods* (3rd ed.). Thousand Oaks, CA: Sage Publications.

Pezzullo, T. R., & Brittingham, B. E. (1993). Characteristics of donors. In M. J. Worth (Ed.), *Educational fund raising: Principles and practice* (pp. 31-38). Phoenix, AZ: The American Council on Education and The Oryx Press.

Rhodes, F. H. (1997). Introduction. In F. H. Rhodes (Ed.), *Successful fund raising for higher education: The advancement of learning* (pp. xvii-xxiv). Phoenix, AZ: The American Council on Education and The Oryx Press.

Tashakkori, A., & Teddlie, C. (2003). The past and future of mixed methods research: From data triangulation to mixed model designs. In A. Tashakkori and C. Teddlie (Eds.), *Handbook of mixed methods in social and behavioral research* (pp. 671-702). Thousand Oaks, CA: Sage Publications.

Walters, A. K. (2006, June 23). States are flush with cash, but colleges face competition for the money. *The Chronicle of Higher Education.*

Worth, M. J. (1993). The historical overview. In M. J. Worth (Ed.), *Educational fundraising: Principles and practice* (pp. 18-28). Phoenix, AZ: The American Council on Education and The Oryx Press.

Chapter 5
A Mixed Methods Study of the Culture of Athletes at a Division I University

Rick Kroc
University of Arizona

Preliminary Note

This study has been underway for about 18 months, at the time of this writing, but will take another 6 months to complete. The description below, then, is a mix of finished and unfinished activities and analyses. The author would be pleased to provide updates on the current status of the project upon request. A public report about the project and its findings should also be available when the study is completed from the President's Office at the University of Arizona.

Need for the Study

College athletics may be the most publicly visible aspect of American higher education. The incidents, concerns, and scandals that surface so regularly can threaten public confidence and undermine the integrity of a college or university. Each year the stakes seem higher and the controversy greater, placing increasing pressure on college presidents, coaches, faculty, staff, and especially the student-athletes.

Although few people would question the need for studies of intercollegiate athletics, conducting sound, thorough, unbiased research in a super-charged environment that mixes politics, economics, and public visibility presents many challenges. At the University of Arizona (UA), the essential condition that made such research possible was an engaged president with a fundamental commitment to improving athletics, born from a strong belief in the benefits of the athletic experience for most student-athletes. He issued this call for the study:

> As Chair of the NCAA Division I Presidential Task Force on the Future of Intercollegiate Athletics, I have both the opportunity and the responsibility to examine the culture of higher education athletics programs in America. My responsibilities begin at home. My task force experience as well as events at colleges and universities around the country led me to conclude that it is appropriate to examine the environment defined by the culture of high-level athletic competition here at The University of Arizona. At the national level a serious movement to strengthen the academic

experience of student-athletes is well underway. We must examine the presence of any cultural influences here that have the potential of distorting the shared values of academics and athletics in higher education.

This study is intended to be a cultural assessment quite apart from the investigations that occur when the Dean of Students responds to any allegations of violations of our Code of Student Conduct by individual students (including student-athletes) and apart from any investigations of alleged criminal conduct by law enforcement authorities. We seek to improve our understanding of the cultural context in which student-athletes function, and to find ways to improve that environment. (Likins, 2005)

The President's involvement with the National Collegiate Athletic Association (NCAA) helped increase the breadth of the study and permit access to NCAA staff and survey materials. For the NCAA, our university study became a pilot project on how research and data (including their nationally administered GOALS survey) can be used to improve the culture of athletics. Their engagement helped strengthen the University's commitment to a sound research project.

Organization and Process
In a study with a high level of controversy and visibility, process and organizational issues may be as important as the methodology, so a short description of these issues may be valuable. First, the President chose two co-principal investigators (PIs) to direct a study that would follow the principles of good social science research. Both had social science research backgrounds as well as extensive administrative experience, one as a dean, the other as a vice president. This set the foundation for a study that would have the credibility of independent research, but would also be oriented toward practical, workable recommendations for improvements.

Second, the PIs and President selected members for the Intercollegiate Athletics Environment Panel (AEP), the group tasked with accomplishing their objectives. The AEP comprised faculty, staff, student, and community representatives. Although the AEP was ultimately responsible to the President and the Arizona Board of Regents, its work was also conducted in close consultation with an Advisory Board consisting of senior University administrators.

This organizational structure ensured that adequate review and oversight of the study occurred, but also meant that considerable time and attention was needed for meetings and process issues. Some efficiency had to be sacrificed for the sake of maintaining adequate communication, review, and support. A two-year timeline and budget was established for the project. The budget included half-time graduate research assistant support for the principal investigators.

Finally, the University was undergoing its NCAA accreditation review while the AEP study was underway. Care was taken to completely separate the AEP study from the accreditation process and self-study. Otherwise, the exigencies of the accreditation needs might well have overwhelmed the AEP goals.

Focus of the Study

The study was divided into two phases. Phase I, mostly quantitative in nature, was designed to look somewhat broadly at the two fundamental study areas:

- Student athletes' academic experience; and
- Student athletes' culture and environment.

Using qualitative methods, Phase II was designed to dig more deeply into the critical issues identified from Phase I. Detailed, targeted recommendations would be developed from these two phases. The following two sets of research questions were designed to guide the study.

Student Athletes' Academic Experience

Is the student-athlete academic experience similar or dissimilar to that of the general student population, and is there sufficient and appropriate support to enhance student-athlete success?

1. Are we doing enough to develop the academic talents and diverse interests of our student athletes?
2. Are student athletes sufficiently integrated into the academic community to ensure their development as educated citizens of the world?
3. Can our academic support systems be improved? Are our academic advisers and student athlete counselors (Committed to an Athlete's Total Success - CATS) meeting the needs of student athletes?
4. What are we doing to address any academic issues identified through our Athletics Progress Report?

Student Athletes' Culture and Environment

Is there evidence of inappropriate behavior that is symptomatic of problems embedded within the culture of UA competition?

1. Are there characteristics (either positive or negative) differentiating

student athletes, the student body, and the larger society regarding behaviors/attitudes related to alcohol/drugs, dishonesty, gambling, racism, sex, sexism, violence, and weapons?

2. If not, is any such inappropriate behavior instead symptomatic of problems more broadly embedded in society?

These questions were written to systematically address local, regional, and national "hot button" issues in intercollegiate Division I athletics. As is evident in the questions, some of these issues are broad, controversial, and often plagued with a preponderance of headline-making, anecdotal data. To grapple with the wide scope of the research questions, a few guiding principles were adopted:

* In every way possible, this research study should be insulated from the politics, biases, and public scrutiny that usually surrounds intercollegiate athletics;
* No single method or data source is definitive—triangulation on a finding using multiple sources is most likely to be valid;
* Quantitative and qualitative methods are both essential: quantitative methods provide broader, more generalizable results, whereas qualitative methods provide depth, context, and understanding.
* Whenever possible, findings about athletes should be compared with data from non-athletes;
* A review of the national literature as well as studies done at other universities or agencies should be used to help shape the study and to provide context for our local findings; and
* No reports should be issued prior to the completion of the study and a subsequent thorough review by the President.

Study Domain: Areas and Populations

The first step in the study was to specify the domain. Beginning from the research questions, the AEP identified more specific areas for study within each of the broad categories of student-athlete's academic experience and their culture/environment. In addition, a graduate research assistant compiled and summarized the national research literature, as well as studies done by the NCAA and by other universities to ensure that the domain was appropriately defined, and that the AEP had knowledge about the array of methods, instruments, and findings that were available. The final list of areas is displayed in Table 1 (next page).

Having identified the content domain, attention turned toward the study population. If media reports were the only source of data, it would appear that athletes misbehave much more frequently than other students. To confirm or disconfirm this appearance, though, requires more systematic, unbiased comparisons between athletes and non-athletes, as well as considerations

Table 1
Domain of the Study

Athlete's academic experience	Athlete's culture and environment
Academic preparation	Alcohol and drugs
Progress to degree	Dishonesty and cheating
Student engagement	Gambling
Academic support	Racism
Post-eligibility academic experience	Sexism
Other academic issues	Sexual behavior
	Violence
	Weapons

of possible explanatory variables such as gender, socio-economic background, academic preparation, race/ethnicity, and sport.

The AEP also agreed at the study outset that the focus would be on NCAA recruited student-athletes. "Walk-on" athletes, who receive no athletic financial aid, would not be including in the study.

Methodology

In very broad terms, the AEP study was distilled into three questions.

1. At this university, are athletes' academic and cultural experiences unique in important ways?
2. If they are unique, why? Can we understand and explain this uniqueness?
3. If we discover problems with athletes, what improvements can we make? If we discover advantages, can we somehow export these advantages to non-athletes?

In some ways this research was more like an evaluation study because the interest was more in the local situation than in any general conclusions that would be relevant to other universities It should be noted, though, that the AEP had no reason to think that the situation at this university was substantively different from other Division I university settings.

Moreover, if we think of athletics as a program to be evaluated, then this study had both formative and summative aspects: the interests were both in systematic identification of "program effects" and in program improvements. Probably more than any other aspect of the study, this concern with both summative and formative issues was the primary trigger for adopting a mixed-method approach.

Phase I—Quantitative

The fundamental aim of this phase was to determine if there were differences between athletes and other students in the areas specified in Table 1. Whenever possible, comparisons by gender, ethnicity, SES, and sport were to be made. The AEP compiled a list of all existing sources of student data that might be relevant, which turned out to be fairly extensive:

- Board of Regents and NCAA reports on athletes' grades and graduation rates (ten year history);
- Institutional student records data;
- Health and Wellness Survey, administered annually to assess student alcohol, drug, and sexual behaviors (seven year history);
- Dean of Students Code of Conduct and Code of Academic Integrity violations (five year history);
- Coalition on Intercollegiate Athletics (COIA) report, completed in 1995; and
- Annual University Survey of Graduating Seniors, assessing student engagement, satisfaction, and other academic issues (five year history).

Each of these sources contained relevant data that could be used to compare athletes with non-athletes and, at least in some cases, break out sub-populations. Only data from and about students was included in this phase of the study.

The AEP was convinced, though, that better coverage of the issues was needed. All of the existing sources had flaws, including small numbers of athletes, inability to break out subpopulations, dated information, and incomplete coverage of the study issues. In addition, one of the guiding principles was triangulation using multiple sources and methods. The AEP decided, then, that new data needed to be collected.

Coincidental with the timing of this study, the NCAA began administering a survey to athletes at Division I universities. This survey, titled Growth, Opportunities, Aspirations, and Learning in College Survey (GOALS) consisted of seven components:

- college athletics experience;
- college academic experience;
- college social experience;

- the student-athlete experience;
- health and well-being;
- time commitments; and
- background information.

Both the NCAA and the University saw opportunities to benefit from a collaboration involving the GOALS survey. For the University, the survey could greatly enhance our understanding of the study issues. The NCAA saw a significant opportunity to have UA serve as a pilot and pioneer in using the survey for our internal needs, particularly as we strive to improve the culture and experiences of student athletes. This proved to be an ideal partnership.

In return for access to the University's GOALS data, the NCAA agreed to scan the completed surveys and provide the data file to the AEP. Further, they realized that having a complementary survey for student non-athletes would serve their needs as well as ours, so they agreed to modify the GOALS for the general student body and provide the new survey to the University for administration during the study.

Because the GOALS survey did not cover most of the culture and environment areas listed in Table 1, the AEP developed supplemental survey questions to be appended to the GOALS survey, both for the athletes and non-athletes. A few University-specific questions about academic issues were also added. The GOALS and the supplemental questions were administered at the same time.

Because the NCAA would have access to our data, it was necessary to obtain human subjects approval from our Institutional Review Board (IRB), which proved to be a time-consuming process, particularly since the domain of the study included some very sensitive and controversial areas. Eventually, approval was obtained, provided the following agreements were honored.

1. The NCAA could have access to the university GOALS data, but not data from the supplemental questions (which covered the controversial areas).
2. Survey responses must be strictly anonymous.
3. Participation must be voluntary.
4. All participants must see (but would not need to sign) an informed consent form with the specific wording that had been approved by the IRB.

Survey administration created some challenges. For the athletes, a paper administration was determined to be most desirable. First, the GOALS survey was only available in a paper format. Second, to achieve a sufficient number of responses from the athletes to parse the data by gender and sport, the AEP felt it best to ask the athletes the come to a central location at times arranged around their academic and practice schedules. Through the President, Athletic Director, and team captains, coaches were strongly encouraged to stress the importance of the survey to their athletes, stopping short, though, of coercing their participation. Several survey administration times were arranged during early mornings, lunch hours, and evenings. Though the AEP's first thought had been to have coaches present, the University Testing Center staff, a neutral group, administered the survey to avoid any appearance of coercion. All student-athletes were invited; 55% participated.

For non-athletes, however, the AEP decided on a web administration. First, the institutional research office routinely develops, administers, and tabulates web surveys, so the technology and infrastructure were robust. Second, this mode would be more efficient and cost effective. These advantages were thought to outweigh any potential bias introduced by using a different mode from the athletes' survey. The GOALS and supplemental questions were converted for the web, and emails were sent to the sample with the URL included in the text. Clicking on the URL brought up both the informed consent language and the survey questions. The email was sent to a random sample of 5,000 non-athlete undergraduates, not including African Americans. Because African Americans are a large part of the student-athlete population, but a small proportion of non-athletes, all non-athlete African American undergraduates were invited to participate. Several $100 gift certificates for the bookstore were offered to randomly selected respondents as incentives. The response rate, 17%, was disappointing, but provided sufficient numbers of respondents for the desired comparisons.

The AEP addressed the value of statistical significance testing of the survey results. Although the focus was primarily on triangulation across methods and on practical significance, statistical significance and confidence intervals were thought to be valuable tools to help sift through the massive number of survey questions, particularly as they were broken out for sub-populations. The reader/analyst could, then, have in mind both the difference that reached various levels of statistical significance and the difference between means that seemed important from a practical standpoint. It was clear, though, that reliance on statistical significance testing would need to be tempered by the potential bias in the representativeness of respondents and in the small sample sizes in some sub-populations.

From the new and existing Phase I data, a detailed profile of student athletes was developed. For further triangulation and a wider context, this profile was compared and contrasted with the national research literature and with other studies, including NCAA studies. These profiles and comparisons were merged into a document titled *Phase I Emerging Profile of Student Athletes (Emerging Profile)*, which became the springboard for Phase II.

Phase II—Qualitative

Guided by the findings from Phase I, Phase II was designed to achieve a deeper, richer understanding of the underlying issues, context, and motivation within the athletic culture—aimed ultimately toward any improvements that might be recommended for the intercollegiate athletics program at the University. The *Emerging Profile* helped shape the domain of the Phase II efforts by identifying those areas where athletes differed from non-athletes in important ways. Moreover, it helped sort out differences by gender and, to some extent, by sport and ethnicity. The small sample sizes in many sports and for some ethnic groups, however, made it impossible to profile many sports and some ethnic groups.

The *Emerging Profile* also helped identify areas that would not be pursued in Phase II. Given the enormous territory covered by the research questions, this sharpened focus was essential to completing the study within the two-year timeframe. Significant differences between athletes and non-athletes with regard to sexism and racism, for example, were not found on this campus in the Phase I data, so were not considered directly in the Phase II domain.

Had Phase I not revealed any important differences between athletes and non-athletes (highly unlikely in light of the national literature and the experiences of many other universities), the study would probably have been concluded at that point. Because there were many differences, though, a clear need to achieve a greater understanding of the underlying issues, the context, and the various stakeholder perspectives was apparent. Phase I only scratched the surface of many areas of the study and gathered primarily only student-level data.

The AEP shifted gears in Phase II from quantitative to qualitative methods and epistemology. For some AEP members, this was a significant educational process. Although everyone has some understanding of focus groups, this understanding is often superficial. Focus groups are often thought of as more like face-to-face surveys where you get a little more information and serve pizza and soft drinks. Questions often arose, for example, about how the "sample" in a focus group would be representative of the population: some thought that each focus group should have a random sample participating. Some AEP members gained an understanding of the differences between methods, whereas others simply decided to trust the process and the "experts." To achieve the thick description, the richer understanding, and the contextual knowledge that was essential for this qualitative phase, it became necessary to expand the information gathered considerably beyond the student-level view used in the mostly quantitative Phase I. Table 2 shows the groups and methods for Phase II.

Shaping the questions for the focus groups and interviews, as well as the characteristics of the participants in the focus groups, was necessary to

Table 2
Populations and Methods for Qualitative Phase

	Focus Groups	Interviews	Follow-up Survey
Students (athletes and non-athletes)	X		X
Athletic advisors	X		If needed
Faculty		X	If needed
Administrators		X	If needed
Coaches		X	If needed

maximize the benefits while minimizing the cost and time. Again, Phase I findings helped with this.

- Survey data clearly indicated that most student-athletes, especially females, clearly benefited from their participation in athletics, so focus group and interview questions were tailored to gain an understanding of this finding from the perspective of (and in the words of) the athletes themselves. In light of some other findings that were clearly negative, the AEP felt that this positive story needed to be told.
- The campus has been administering the Health and Wellness Survey, which collects detailed data on alcohol and drug behavior, for seven years. The rich information available about athletes and non-athletes from this survey meant that there was a minimal need to address these areas in Phase II. This illustrates how more "quantitative" methods, like surveys, can also gather qualitative data.
- Although much of the Phase I data could not be broken out by sport because of small n's, it was possible to compare revenue-generating sports (men's basketball and football at this university) with other men's sports. Some clear differences between these two groups that emerged from Phase I helped with the development of interview and focus group questions, as well as in the selection of group

participants. The fact that these differences between revenue and non-revenue sports were confounded by differences in ethnicity (athletes in revenue sports are predominately African American) and socio-economic status also helped guide the development of questions. For example, focus group questions were designed to elicit comparisons between the high school culture and the university community culture as experienced by the participating students.

- Ultimately, the data gathered in Phase I resulted in parsing the data and designing Phase II using three fundamental comparisons, stemming from identified differences between:

  - student-athletes and non-athletes;
  - males and females; and
  - revenue-generating men's sports and non-revenue men's sports.

Visually:

		Athletes	Non-Athletes
Women	All sports	X	X
Men	Revenue sport	X	X
	Non-revenue sport	X	X

Phase II data collection began with student focus groups of about 6-10 students each. It was determined that the breadth of issues and the identified differences across populations would require 16 student focus groups, eight for athletes and eight for non-athletes. Each focus group was staffed by a facilitator and a co-facilitator (note taker). The AEP considered recording each session, but decided that this would be too expensive and time-consuming. Facilitators and note takers were identified from campus personnel with care taken to ensure that the staffing of focus groups would maximize the candidness of the students (for example, coaches would be bad choices as facilitators).

A six-page training manual, *Running a Focus Group*, was developed and two training sessions were held for facilitators and note takers. Highlights for the sessions included guidelines for:

- Creating a warm and friendly environment before beginning the focus group;

- Introducing the topic and participants;
- Establishing discussion ground rules, including having every participant sign an informed consent form;
- Asking the opening question, which is designed to be an icebreaker to generate easy conversation;
- Asking the content questions, including tips for listening, probing, and group management;
- Taking notes and summarizing the discussion so that participants have a last chance to talk and clarify their ideas;
- Closing the session, including providing an opportunity to complete a brief follow-up survey (see next paragraph); and
- Completing each session with a discussion between the facilitator and co-facilitator designed to identify issues with the overall session, capture the richness of the discussion, identify main themes, and ensure that key statements and quotes are recorded.

Before each session, facilitators were provided with a written protocol tailored to the specific focus group topic and type of participant. This protocol consisted of:

1. Background information;
2. Purpose of the focus group;
3. Specific questions and possible prompts; and
4. A one-page survey with open-ended questions about the topic. The survey was intended to supplement the focus group conversation, providing a different source of information to confirm (or disconfirm) and amplify issues emerging from the discussion.

Recruitment of student-athlete participants was arranged through the Athletics Compliance Officer, a member of the AEP, who contacted the coaches to arrange voluntary participation. Working around academic and practice schedules was challenging.

Recruitment of non-athletes was done as follows.

1. A sample of 5,000 non-athletes was drawn from the University student database. Because African Americans are statistically overrepresented among athletes, but not many would be captured in the random sample of non-athletes, all additional African American non-athlete students were added to the original sample of 5,000.
2. Emails were sent to these students, asking if they would like to participate (pizza, soda, and their desire to make a difference were the incentives).

3. If they were interested, they were asked to click on a URL, where they would indicate the topics they were interested in, times that they were available, their class level, and gender.
4. An automated process added the interested students to the non-athlete focus groups until 6-10 students were in each group.

Next Steps—Qualitative Phase

At the time of this writing (November, 2006), student focus groups are underway, and plans are being made for other qualitative data collection. In particular, one or two focus groups will be held with the academic advisors assigned to advise only athletes. These staff members, who are professional advisors rather than faculty, have a unique perspective on the culture of athletes, especially (but not only) with regard to academic issues. They may also have constructive ideas for valuable changes.

Coaches are another group with a unique and critical perspective. In many ways, the coach is the pivotal person in an athlete's life during his or her time at the University. It is essential to obtain their views on the issues underlying the culture of athletes and to seek their input about possible improvements. Since there may be a variety of unique circumstances for a particular team, and there are a relatively small number of coaches, interviews were determined to be the best way to gather the needed data. Also, coaches may be more willing to be forthcoming in a one-on-one setting than in a group.

Finally, key faculty and administrators will be selected for interviews. Depending on how clear the findings are from the previous data collection and analysis, these interviews may focus on possible improvements rather than context and underlying issues.

Analysis and Recommendations

Phase II data (notes from focus groups and interviews, as well as responses to open-ended survey questions) will be analyzed using a content analysis approach. Themes will be initially identified, corroborating evidence will be added, and then themes may be modified (or new themes proposed), depending on how "corroborating" the evidence turns out to be. This kind of recursive, feedback-oriented approach should result in a rich, deep understanding of the culture of athletes at this university.

Phase II findings will then be "blended" with Phase I results. In some cases, all data and analyses may point in the same direction. For example, it appears to be clear from Phase I and the initial Phase II student focus groups that excessive alcohol use occurs among student athletes, particularly males. In light of national studies that have reached the same conclusion, this is not a surprising finding. In other areas, though, overall findings may be less clear. It will be interesting, for example, to see what Phase II reveals about physical violence and weapons, areas that were somewhat ambiguous in the Phase I data and analysis.

The AEP has been asked by the President to use the study results to make recommendations for improvements in intercollegiate athletics. These recommendations will come from two sources:

1. Directly by soliciting suggestions from participants during Phase II focus groups, interviews and surveys; and
2. Indirectly from the analysis of the data gathered during both phases and the subsequent AEP discussions.

The Value of a Mixed Methods Approach

The drawbacks of a mixed methods approach are clear: it adds time, complexity, and expense to a study. Some would also say that it mixes methods that are epistemologically contradictory. So what was the value of this approach for this study?

- Athletic culture spans a spectrum of areas, some of which (alcohol use, for example) have become fairly well understood over the years from quantitative methods, others of which (physical violence, weapons use) need the deeper exploration and understanding provided by qualitative methods.
- The formative and summative aspects of this study, which is more like program evaluation in many ways than like a traditional research study, lend themselves to a mixed methods approach.
- Audiences and stakeholders consist of some people who respond best to systematic, inferentially rigorous, quantitative data, but also others who want to hear the complex, richly detailed stories derived from the individuals who are immersed in the culture. Different approaches resonate with different audiences.
- Mixed methods also means that multiple methods have been employed, which is essential to using triangulation as a means to establish greater validity of the findings. Any single approach used in the messy world of social science research will be flawed. If a wide array of methods leads to consistent conclusions, then analysts and stakeholders feel more confident about conclusions and recommendations.

References

Likins, Peter (2005). Call to the intercollegiate athletics environment panel. The University of Arizona. URL: http://web.arizona.edu/~likins/communications/letters/letter19/ (active as of 2/6/07)

Chapter 6
Discovering What Students and Professors Expect From Advising Relationships

Carol Trosset
Hampshire College

Grinnell College, a selective private liberal arts college in central Iowa, is a college that emphasizes advising as central to students' education and as an important responsibility of faculty members. The importance of advising is enhanced by the fact that Grinnell has no distribution requirements, but asks each student to craft his or her own curriculum in consultation with a faculty adviser. During my years as Grinnell's Director of Institutional Research (1995-2004), the college gathered an increasing amount of information evaluating its advising system. These activities culminated in a grant from the Lilly Foundation, focusing partly on the nature and importance of the mentoring process.

The research process described in this chapter, and the resulting analysis, is not a single isolated project. Rather, it should be read as a sequence of projects, each building on the previous ones. A question is posed, data are gathered and analyzed, and the results lead to another question, which requires a different method of gathering and analyzing a different set of data, which leads to a third question, and so on. Therefore, the structure of this chapter will reflect this process, showing not simply a set of questions, a method, and a set of data, but also how each step in the research process was designed, or re-analyzed, to build on the previous findings.

Questions Addressed in the Study

The overarching question motivating all this research was "How good is advising, and what could be done to improve it?" In pursuing this question, I asked many other questions, designed to gain a deeper ethnographic understanding of the advising process. Ethnographic research is a process developed in the field of cultural anthropology, and uses qualitative data (usually from interviews) and in-depth exposure to a community to gain an understanding of the perspectives and assumptions of the community members.

The simplest approach to evaluating the quality of advising is to ask the students about the advising they have received. In 1997, Grinnell College administered the ACT Survey of Academic Advising to a stratified random sample of its students and received responses from a representative third of the student body. (A stratified random sample is one in which subjects are drawn separately from a variety of categories present in the population—such as class year, sex, or ethnicity— but in which individuals within each of those categories has an equal chance of being selected.)

The questions on the ACT Advising survey primarily measure two things: (a) whether students discussed, or wish they had discussed, various topics with their advisers, and (b) their levels of satisfaction with those discussions and with other qualities their advisers may or may not have possessed. Here are some of the results we obtained on this and on another survey:

- 67% said the advising system met their needs "well" or "exceptionally well."
- 76% of seniors were very or generally satisfied with first-year advising.
- 88% of seniors were very or generally satisfied with major advising.
- On a 1-5 scale, with 5 being *strongly agree*, students gave the following average responses:
  - "My adviser encourages me to take an active role in planning my academic program" = 4.4.
  - "My adviser respects my right to make my own decisions" = 4.4.
  - "My adviser is flexible in helping me plan my academic program" = 4.3.
  - "My adviser is a helpful, effective, adviser whom I would recommend to other students" = 4.1.

This was all good news, confirmed by national norms showing that these were relatively high numbers.

Therefore, the first question I had to ask was, "Is student satisfaction a good and valid measure of the quality of advising?" In particular, when students are satisfied (or dissatisfied), what is it they are satisfied (or dissatisfied) *with*? Are they satisfied with the kind of things that faculty members and administrators think that students should want? Are students' expectations of advising in agreement with the kinds of help and guidance that faculty advisers are trying to provide? And we must not assume that all students want the same thing—this is something that can, and should, be described empirically. If different students want different things from advisers, what are the various types of student advisees and what does each type of student want? Finally, how do students (of different types) actually behave in an advising relationship?

Now, as with other features of the educational process, the student perspective is an essential component but not the only one. To understand advising, I also needed to study the experiences of faculty advisers. This involved posing a similar set of questions:

- What kinds of advising are faculty members trying to provide?
- What do faculty advisers expect of themselves and of students?
- Are all faculty advisers trying to provide the same thing?
- What makes a faculty adviser satisfied or dissatisfied with advising a particular student?
- Do faculty members draw a distinction between "advising" and "mentoring"? If so, do different faculty members draw the same distinction?

Finally, as I sought to answer all these questions, I tried to frame my research in ways that would result in practical information that a college could use to facilitate more effective advising for a greater number of students.

Project #1: Interviews with Seniors
Finding out about student perceptions of advising in any kind of detail clearly required interviews with a number of students. Gathering a large number of interviews required more than one interviewer. So in Spring 2003, I directed a group of anthropology students in a study of student views of advising. In an Ethnographic Research Methods course, we designed and tested the interview questions, decided how to draw a sample of students to interview, and then collected interviews with 42% of the 2003 senior class. We asked about their experiences of advising: with their first-year adviser, with their major adviser, and with other adults from whom they had sought advice during college.

Table 1 shows the seven types of interaction with advisers that I was able to identify by reviewing the interview notes collected by the student interviewers. How students perceived these types of interaction varied from one student to another—that is, some students wanted guidance with their academic planning, while others wanted to be left alone.

I was still wondering whether good advising resulted in satisfied

Table 1
Types of Positive Student Interaction

Types of Positive Interaction (from student interviews)
Adviser solves logistical problems (scheduling conflicts, etc.)
Adviser helps with academic difficulties
Adviser encourages curricular breadth
Adviser guides student's academic planning
Adviser helps plan future after college
Personal relationship with adviser
Adviser leaves student alone

students, so I tried to sort out the relationship between what an individual student experienced and whether s/he was satisfied or dissatisfied. I used my knowledge of faculty and administration values to decide whether a student had described "good" or "weak" advising. "Good advising" was considered to include serious discussion of a student's academic goals, course selection, and other related issues, while "weak advising" was defined by the apparent absence of these features. These counts, of course, are tentative and approximate, because not every interview collected enough detail to permit such a characterization. Even with sufficient detail, I cannot know whether the description given in the interview was an accurate description of the advising relationship. However, it seemed worth investigating whether students who *said* they had received the kind of advising the college attempts to provide were more satisfied than those who said they had not.

Table 2 shows that the relationship between satisfaction and the apparent quality of advising is more complex than we might wish.

Table 2
Satisfaction and Apparent Quality

Apparent Quality of Advising Received	Student's Retrospective Assessment
23 described having received good advising.	19 were satisfied
	4 were dissatisfied, saying they wanted a more personal relationship with the adviser.
18 described having received some good and some weak advising.	18 had mixed feelings.
9 described having received weak advising.	8 were dissatisfied.
	1 was satisfied.
19 said that they had not wanted or sought advice.	17 were satisfied.
	2 regretted this in retrospect.

Project #2: Identifying Types of Advisees

Clearly I needed to unpack the advising experience further, to get a useful picture of what was really going on. In Spring 2004, I turned to a pre-existing data set that had been gathered for a completely different purpose: the surveys of current and former advisees that Grinnell does for faculty members going through third-year, tenure, or promotion reviews. I was able to work with the results of surveys concerning 35 different faculty members. By doing a content analysis of what things different students praised or criticized about their advisers, I was able to identify three *types* of advisees (see Table 3), who appear to want very different things from the advising relationship. A description of the types is followed by sample quotes—some of these come from the surveys, and others from the interviews conducted during Project #1.

Table 3
Types of Advisees

TYPES OF ADVISEES	CHARACTERISTICS
ENGAGED	Seeks advice, wants adviser to make the student think things through.
PASSIVE	Wants attention and suggestions, but no pressure; thinks adviser should initiate contact, find and provide all information, and prevent the student from making any mistakes.
RESISTANT	Wants to make all their own decisions without interference; thinks advisers should not have opinions or disagree with students; advisers should sign pre-registration cards but otherwise leave students alone.

Quotes by ENGAGED advisees:

- "He challenges me to take courses in unfamiliar areas, so that my education is balanced. He's helped me tremendously with my four-year plan."
- "While thinking about what I want to do with my time here, she always pushes me to see how each class fits into my long-term goals."
- "She helped me decide which classes to take, how I could incorporate my concentration into post-graduate plans related to my major."

Quotes by PASSIVE advisees:

- "My advisor has been really lenient with me choosing classes for my major. He's let me do whatever I want and take whatever I want to. However, he didn't tell me what I would have wanted to know. I wish I hadn't taken some of the classes I took. He should have asked me more about my post-graduation goals so we could have designed my schedule to better fit what I want to do after I graduate."
- "If there was a question he couldn't answer, he always did the leg-work for me, making phone calls and looking on the internet, then giving me the pertinent information."
- "She was okay, except that I arranged all but maybe one appointment."

Quotes by RESISTANT advisees:

- "I like the freedom he gives for course selection; if Grinnell says it has an open curriculum it should not worry about distribution."

- "I have always been very independent when it comes to course selection, so we did not discuss these things."
- "We occasionally disagreed on courses and I once changed my schedule after she signed my card to include a class I wanted but she was against."
- "I never talked to my tutorial prof ["tutorial" is the first-year seminar class for which the professor serves as the student's pre-major adviser], just looked for a rubber stamp on the classes I was taking. I picked my major adviser based on a rumor that this prof would let me take whatever classes I wanted. Same thing when I declared my second major—just found a professor who would approve whatever I wanted. I never had much interaction with professors."
- "He's a good advisor—he's really open and doesn't care what I take."

The advising described by the "engaged" students is just the sort of thing the college tries to cultivate. It also seems likely that colleges tend to assume that students want that sort of advising. But the comments provided by the "resistant" students show us that not all students want their advisers to make suggestions and challenge their thinking. Whether or not these latter students are accurately describing what went on, it is clear that some students do not want to discuss their academic decisions with a professor.

Project #3: Faculty Views of Advising

In light of these varied descriptions of student desires and experiences, it is clearly important to learn how faculty members experience advising relationships. Grinnell faculty members hold a variety of views of their own roles in the "open curriculum." Some believe they should be very assertive in trying to influence each student's choices. Others believe the college has essentially told them that they do not have the right to refuse to sign a student's card, that once the adviser has told the student what he or she thinks, the adviser should approve whatever the student decides. And some have moved from the first position to the second over time, after seeing students switch advisers in order to find someone who will let them do whatever they want.

Grinnell's published rationale for the open curriculum is that having students make all their own choices fosters student responsibility. On the 1998 Higher Education Research Institute (HERI) faculty survey, we added a local question asking faculty members to agree or disagree with the following statement: "The lack of curricular requirements is an effective way to foster the growth of student responsibility." Respondents were split 50-50 on this question. There were no patterns identified when the responses were analyzed by rank, sex, or discipline.

In Spring 2002, I conducted interviews with 28 faculty members (about 25% of the tenured and tenure-track faculty) about their experiences of advising students. I asked them to relate stories of successful and unsuccessful advising encounters, and to discuss what good advising requires of them, and what things make it difficult. The stratified random sample, including about 25% of tenured and tenure-track faculty members, was representative of gender, rank, and academic division, none of which correlated with any of the responses given.

Let me begin with the stories interviewees told about good or successful advising encounters. The types of stories show what kinds of things happen in effective advising relationships.

- Matching a student with an outside opportunity, such as a summer internship or a graduate program.
- Increasing a student's self-confidence and awareness of opportunities.
- Helping overly focused students to broaden their curricular choices.
- Helping students discover their own interests and priorities by helping them think about why they like or dislike a certain subject, the advantages and disadvantages of a certain major, or their reasons for considering graduate study.
- Convincing students to challenge themselves, for example by urging them to complete Phi Beta Kappa requirements, take a course the student will find difficult, or attend off-campus study in an unfamiliar environment.
- Helping a student sort out the logistics of a program, such as planning a double major.
- Mediating between a student and a classroom professor, usually by convincing the student to talk to the professor.
- Supporting a student who is going through personal difficulties, by listening, providing information about support services, and advocating for the student within the college.

Based on these and related stories, there appear to be seven main types of positive advising interactions: helping with logistics, trouble-shooting academic problems, helping students discover their own interests and priorities, helping overly focused students to broaden, convincing students to challenge themselves, helping students plan for the future, and supporting students in personal difficulties. As shown in Table 4, the success stories fell into categories that roughly matched the types of positive interactions described by students. Note that no students mentioned an adviser convincing students to challenge themselves, and no faculty member mentioned leaving students alone—at least not as a positive thing.

Table 4
Faculty and Student Views of Position Interaction

Types of Positive Interaction – student interviews	Types of Positive Interaction – faculty interviews
Adviser solves logistical problems	Help with logistics
Adviser helps with academic difficulties	Trouble-shoot academic difficulties
Adviser encourages curricular breadth	Help overly focused students to broaden
	Convince students to challenge themselves
Adviser guides student's academic planning	Help students discover own interests and priorities
Adviser helps plan future after college	Help students plan for the future, match students with outside opportunities
Personal relationship with adviser	Support a student in personal difficulties
Adviser leaves student alone	

Advisers were also asked what good advising requires of them. Their collective wisdom seems worth repeating here.

- Know about the student's goals, background, personality, strengths, weaknesses, and assumptions. This knowledge enables the adviser to figure out what makes sense for that student as an individual, rather than just fitting everyone into a general model, and to help them fit what they want to do academically with all the nonacademic things they also want to do.
- Know the institution's programs and requirements, the options available and the timing needed to do particular things, so the adviser can suggest things that would respond to the student's individual talents and interests.
- Have a genuine appreciation of the liberal arts makes it easier to explain why students should want to learn about a variety of fields and to consider subjects that would be beneficial or of interest to a particular student.
- Knowledge of the world outside the institution enables advisers to make students aware of, and help match them with, jobs, internships, and graduate programs. (One respondent said this is where advisers often fail, especially when the student is not going on to graduate school.)
- Establish good rapport with students so they will talk openly. Then be a good listener, pay attention, and make sure of understanding

what they say. Be willing to ask students questions, and help them learn to listen to themselves.
- Take a genuine interest in the students. To be effective, an adviser must want what's best for them, and be able to know the difference between one's own wants and regrets, and what applies to that particular student. This includes being willing and able to care about people without necessarily liking them. It helps, one person said, to start by assuming the best about students, that their intentions are good, that problems are real and not just due to laziness.
- Use one's knowledge of the student to think about how appropriate the student's goals and plans are for them. The adviser should make the student both secure and insecure, get them to confront both their strengths and their weaknesses. Sometimes it's necessary to say things the student doesn't want to hear, to be frank and not gloss over a student's weaknesses or unrealistic plans.
- Staying in touch with students during the semester, preferably face-to-face, because advising takes time.

The success stories in Table 4 appear to refer either to engaged advisees, or sometimes to passive advisees who gradually became more engaged. But various challenges were also mentioned: advising underachievers and students with academic difficulties, dealing with students who don't want advice, and finding appropriate solutions in cases where there are conflicting faculty expectations within a department or program. In addition, one respondent remarked that for good advising to work, something is required of the student also: The student must have an open mind and take an interest in what the adviser has to say. Table 5 shows how the problems described by faculty members are related to the passive and resistant types of advisees.

Table 5
Advising Problems Encountered by Faculty Members

PASSIVE	RESISTANT	ROLE CONFUSION
Students who can't make choices or decisions	Students who don't want to be advised	Being a demanding professor while being a supportive adviser
	Students who avoid certain subjects	Students who want help with personal problems
Students who won't plan ahead or get organized	Students with unrealistic goals who won't reconsider them	
	Students who want special treatment	
Under-achieving students who don't seek help	Students who don't want to be challenged	

Back to Project #2: Types of Advising Relationships

Advising is not the only context in which students talk about wanting more "personal," non-academic, contact with professors. Sometimes in interviews or surveys, students refer to a certain professor as a "good friend," or claim that a particular relationship is "very close." Without more details, we don't know what this means—what they think they want, what they think they have, or whether it's what the professor thinks they have.

Reading descriptions in surveys and interviews made it possible for me to describe types of "personal" interaction. Note that the words used by students (such as "a good friend") do not permit us to determine which type is being described. Table 6 characterizes three types of perception and is followed by student quotes illustrating the thinking behind each type.

Table 6
Types of Personal Interaction

TYPES OF PERSONAL INTERACTION	CHARACTERISTICS
GOOD RAPPORT	Professor greets student on/off campus; they occasionally chat about non-academic things.
ADVISER AS CONFIDANT	Student tells professor about private/personal life; professor listens and/or takes an active interest.
ADVISER AS BUDDY	Student wants to hang out and socialize as with a same-age friend (rare).

Good Rapport

- "I have a really good relationship with both advisors. I know the names and ages of their children, and they know just as much about me."
- "I've run into him at the farmers' market with his family several times. He's always said hello and asked how my classes were going."
- "Particularly meaningful to me is her true interest in me. After coming back from summer break she greeted me and asked me about my summer and so forth. It is nice to have a prof know you as a person."

Adviser as Confidant

- "He was a wonderful adviser; I could talk over anything that was bothering me, whether or not it related to academics."
- "She is like my parent away from home; always there, always listening, and always bursting with fantastic and honest advice."
- "The strength of the advising I've received here is how great my

advisor is. He's really approachable and down-to-earth and fatherly. I really feel comfortable talking to him. We have conversations that aren't just about academics. I've told him things about my family, about my personal relationships, and about some really intimate, personal things. He is one of the very few faculty members that I have shared that kind of information with."

Adviser as Buddy

- "I really like non-academic relations with profs, just hanging out with them."
- "I became great friends with my major advisor; we hang out together on weekends."

A large number of students who mentioned wanting, or liking, having a personal relationship with an adviser simply meant the type of good rapport described in the first set of quotes. At least at small residential colleges, this type of interaction is generally expected and happens frequently. The faculty advisers who behave in this way would probably not use phrases like "close" or "a good friend" to describe how they relate to these students, and we must not over-interpret the claims of students who use those terms.

Obviously, there are possible personal complications that could result from the "confidant" and "buddy" models. And the confidant role is one that some faculty members embrace and others avoid. While the "good rapport" model might form part of the expectations of faculty members at some types of colleges, it seems unlikely that the "confidant" model is ever considered part of the faculty adviser's job description. With respect to "hanging out," we should again remember that the faculty member might describe the situation differently. One colleague at another institution told me that he often goes to the campus coffee shop to read or grade papers. Sometimes, he said, a student from one of his classes will sit down and chat with him for five or ten minutes. He said it would never occur to him to describe this as "hanging out," but that it seems possible that the student might think of it that way.

There are also some potential *academic* complications that can arise from different perceptions of the meaning of the personal dimension of advising relationships. For example, I have heard occasional anecdotes from faculty members about students who seemed unable to believe that a professor would actually give them a D in a course. This disbelief appeared to come from the students having been told to think of professors as supportive friends, and acting as if they thought "friends don't give friends a D." They reported that these students acted as if no failure on their part could result in a D or an F, since this would impede their progress in the major, and the college had told them "we want you to succeed."

Project #4: Student Curricular Choices

Grinnell has the same goals for curricular breadth as do liberal arts institutions with extensive distribution requirements. The catalog recommends that all students take courses in all three divisions—humanities, social studies, and sciences—as well as writing, mathematics, and foreign language courses. There is a cap on the number of credits that may be taken in any one division (Grinnell College 2003-2005 Academic Catalog, page 22).

In the mid 1990s, and again in 2004, I conducted large-scale transcript analysis projects. I found that 84% of the last five years of graduates had taken three courses in each division. Whether that sounds high or low depends on your point of view. Some people argued that, for a voluntary act, this was quite high and very satisfactory. Others pointed out that if we had requirements it would be 100%. Our 1998 re-accreditation self-study reported that "The majority of Grinnell College students take a reasonable distribution of courses across the three academic divisions."

The most common "deficit" occurs when humanities majors take fewer than three science courses. In the spring of 1997, I interviewed 18 such students to ask their reasons. These interviews took place during the students' final semester before graduation, so that they could not be perceived as pressuring the students to make different choices. Students were asked what science courses they had taken, why they had chosen it/ them, why they had not taken more science courses, and whether they had done any math or science at other institutions during the summers.

Only one had transferred science credit from another institution. One other claimed a math learning disability. Ten said they had arrived at Grinnell knowing they were not interested in science and did not want to take any. Nine said math and science had been hard for them in high school. Many had negative (mis)perceptions of science: as uncreative with no room for new ideas, as cold and distant and unconcerned about people, as very specialized and unrelated to their lives, and as pointless for anyone not planning a scientific career. Several disliked labs or thought they took up too much time.

Why is this project part of a study of advising? Because fully half of these students said they had actively resisted pressure from their advisers to take more science. We learn three things about advising from these interviews. First, we validate the existence of the category of "resistant advisees." Second, we gain independent evidence confirming the faculty interviews in which advisers described students who avoid certain subjects and do not want to be challenged. Third, we now have a clear illustration of the difference between students receiving advice and being influenced by it. This last distinction raises additional questions about what we mean by good advising: is it defined simply by the actions of the adviser, or also by the receptiveness of the student?

Project #5: Advisee Type and Curricular Choice

The next question, it seemed, was whether the different types of advisees made better or worse curricular choices. I made an initial attempt to answer this question, using the Project #1 interviews with 122 seniors about their experiences of advising and linking their interviews with their transcript records. Based on their comments, I was able to "type" about half of the students interviewed, with a reasonable degree of confidence. Table 7 shows what percent of each advisee type fulfilled the unofficial standard for a well-distributed curriculum at Grinnell: three courses each in humanities/ arts, natural sciences, and social sciences.

Given the small sample sizes, these numbers are *not* significant. All we can really say at this point is that there is no clear and obvious connection between the type of advisee and their curricular breadth. One important missing variable is the type of adviser each student had.

Table 7
Course Distribution by Advisee Type

Advisee Type	N=	Took 3+ courses in each division
Engaged	11	73%
Passive	32	81%
Resistant	12	83%
Unclassified	59	80%

Project #6: Types of Professors

At this point, I retrieved data I had collected in 1995, when I had interviewed 35 tenured and tenure-track Grinnell professors. These interviews were not specifically about advising; instead they included thirteen scenarios about faculty-student interaction. Each interviewee was asked to rate each scenario on the appropriateness of the action taken in it. The following six scenarios had proved useful in differentiating between different views of appropriate types of faculty-student interaction.

- A professor follows a policy of lowering the grades of students who repeatedly miss class or come late.
- A professor refuses to accept a late assignment, on the grounds that the student had not requested an extension and that his/her only reason for being late was a heavy workload.
- A professor notices that a student who did badly on the last test has been missing class. He or she tries repeatedly to contact the student to find out what the problem is.
- A student goes to a professor to discuss a personal problem.

- A professor, when invited, attends student parties on campus.
- A student frequently addressed professors by their first names, without being asked to do so.

Table 8 shows the three models of faculty/student interaction that emerged from a cluster analysis of the 35 sets of responses.

ROLE-DISTANT PROFESSORS accounted for 16 of the 35 faculty members interviewed. More than half were assistant professors. Some quotes:

Table 8
Faculty Types

TYPES OF PROFESSORS	CHARACTERISTICS
ROLE-DISTANT	Sees attendance and deadlines as the student's responsibility and consequences are appropriate; limited outreach is okay but not required; students should take personal problems elsewhere; would only attend formal group events (like ethnic club dinners); no first names.
FLEXIBLE	Should be flexible regarding attendance and deadlines; outreach is appropriate; student should notify professor if a personal problem is affecting academic work but should get help elsewhere; social distance is important but details of interaction can vary.
NURTURING	Should encourage/require attendance but be flexible about deadlines; outreach is good; the confidant role is appropriate; some social informality is okay.

- "The syllabus has every due date; it's the student's job to get the work done."
- "If you said 'no extensions' in advance, then it would not be fair to the rest of the class to make an exception."
- "Discussing personal problems with students is fraught with difficulties. I've become very efficient at referring them elsewhere to deal with complex problems."
- "I hope professors and students can be friendly, but being friends has to wait until after graduation, not before."

FLEXIBLE PROFESSORS accounted for 11 individuals, many of them full professors. From the available data, we cannot be sure whether we are observing a generational difference, or whether the flexible style is a learned behavior.

- "Attendance is usually a moot point—those students do so badly you don't need to dock their grades."
- "We ought to be more flexible about late work, even though we get taken advantage of sometimes."
- "When they tell me about problems, they usually have implications for class. If they came with lots of irrelevant problems, I'd say that was not appropriate."
- "I don't have strong feelings about using names – as long as the students don't want to 'hang out'."

NURTURING PROFESSORS accounted for eight individuals. They occurred evenly across ranks, and—contrary to student-held stereotypes—seem more likely to be male than female.

- "I'm Mr. Softie—I always accept late work."
- "I always try to contact students who are having trouble—it takes a lot of time."
- "Sometimes we can help with their problems."
- "If the students want us there (at parties), we should go."
- "I encourage students to use my first name."

Assuming that these general approaches to faculty-student interaction will affect how professors approach the advising relationship, we can speculate about how different combinations of student and faculty types might work out. Table 9 is as yet unsupported by data, but could be tested if enough were known about the individuals in particular advising relationships.

These types of interaction would probably apply to any type of interaction that goes beyond a student simply taking a class: advising, research collaboration, coaching in athletics or fine arts, or any other type of intensive ongoing relationship. Using advising as a general model, Engaged students will probably do well anywhere that they can *get* good

Table 9
Matching Student and Adviser Types

	ROLE-DISTANT PROFESSOR	FLEXIBLE PROFESSOR	NURTURING PROFESSOR
ENGAGED STUDENT	Success likely	Success likely	Success likely
PASSIVE STUDENT	Both dissatisfied	Success possible	Mutual satisfaction, possibly limited growth
RESISTANT STUDENT	Little interaction	?	Student feels smothered

advice and guidance—and they will certainly thrive at a small college with concerned professors. Passive and Resistant students will doubtless present difficulties for their advisers at any institution. It might be useful to interview experienced flexible professors about how they work with these two types of advisees.

Back to Project #3: Definitions of Advising and Mentoring

Perhaps these differences in types of interaction can be illuminated by the distinction between "advising" and "mentoring." Although these terms are sometimes used interchangeably, all but 5 of the 28 individuals interviewed made a distinction between advising and mentoring. Two different kinds of distinctions were made, and some individuals mentioned both of them. (Those who said advising and mentoring were the same were describing the first type described below.)

One Professor described mentoring as the facilitation of the student's overall personal development. Here advising is seen as very circumscribed, and consists of helping students meet the expectations of the college, suggesting alternatives and encouraging them to explore. The professor shepherds the student's academic program. Advising largely focuses on course choices, and expectations are clearly defined.

Mentoring for personal development is seen as more encompassing. Some describe it as a form of parenting, using the phrase in *loco parentis*. It requires the professor to be a role model and talk to students about life, sharing in their personal growth. It can include helping them with study skills and classroom interactions, and showing them how to deal with particular circumstances. It may or may not be academic in focus. It is defined as a more connected position than advising, with more responsibility, more investment in the relationship. This type of mentoring is more about life in general, concerned with the whole person, helping students with the non-academic things in their lives. The mentor and student become personally close, and the mentor provides a model of how to have a fulfilling life. It takes more time and includes more informal interaction, such as going to see students perform in sports events, plays, or concerts. It is a more personal and more mutual relationship than advising, and has fluid expectations.

The second definition referred to mentoring an incipient colleague. Here "advising" means helping a student do what that student wants to do, when what they want is something different from what the professor does. "Mentoring," on the other hand, of this second type happens when the professor and the student have an intellectual affinity, and the student comes to the professor having already defined him or herself as wanting to do what the professor does, and wanting to learn about it from that person. The student shares the professor's academic interests and professional goals. The mentor sees the student over time, demonstrating how to do something the mentor knows well, providing a model of what a scholar in a particular field is like, how to act and think. This kind of relationship has a strong focus on a particular subject area. The mentor engages with the student at a deep level, in a more sustained, developed, and intense relationship than "advising" requires. Ideally, both people find themselves growing. Mentoring is more hands-on than advising, helping the student emulate what the mentor does. It takes place with some majors, and it happens from day-to-day, in upper-level classes or in research projects. The mentor sees the student fairly regularly and the two work on a specific set of skills. It generally happens in the context of some kind of project.

Proponents of both models of mentoring stressed that some students need and/or want mentoring and some do not. A student who wants to be mentored will seek it out. Mentoring of either type is seen as more organic than advising and as related to personalities; it cannot be planned or assigned. The mentoring of an incipient colleague specifically depends on the student being seriously interested in that particular subject. Either kind of mentoring works by both parties knowing what they want from the relationship and being willing to give it. No one saw mentoring as an institutional responsibility, but as arising out of relationships.

The first type of mentoring, for personal development, would appear to be the preferred model of Nurturing professors. It might work with either an Engaged or a Passive student. Mentoring an incipient colleague would require an Engaged student, but could happen with any of the three types of professors.

Methodological Lessons Learned

Qualitative research methods do much more than simply "provide a voice" for the people we study. Direct quotations are extremely valuable, but their value is increased when we can use them to illustrate points that go beyond what any one person told us. Using appropriate analytical strategies, we can investigate things people say to discover things they assume or value but cannot articulate, and bring them into consciousness.

Gathering appropriate data often means asking questions of subjects that are different from the questions that we, as researchers, are trying to answer. Collecting qualitative data is difficult and time consuming, but most of the work of qualitative research lies in the analysis.

Sometimes valuable information can be gained by viewing things as data sets that were designed for another purpose. Several parts of this study were designed to investigate advising, but useful data were also obtained from evaluations of faculty members seeking promotion or tenure, and from interviews done several years in advance that were not concerned with advising.

Impact of the Study

Although this research did not result in finding out "how good advising is," it did produce a great deal of knowledge that can contribute both to improving advising and evaluating it in more appropriate ways. Knowing about the varied expectations different types of students have of advising could help colleges to avoid the use of simple student satisfaction to evaluate advisers. Going further, this research and these typologies could be used to educate both students and advisers about how to work well together. Awareness of stylistic variations could help teach both groups about appropriate expectations, provide suggestions about how to interact in effective ways, and prepare all participants for challenges they may encounter. In my experience, faculty development workshops on advising tend to focus on how to do a better job with engaged students, but may offer little help in developing effective interactions with passive or resistant advisees. The typologies could also be used to design diagnostic instruments and thereby improve our effectiveness at matching different types of students with appropriate advisers.

Acknowledgements: One set of faculty interviews was funded as part of a grant to Grinnell College from the Lilly Foundation. I also gratefully acknowledge the contributions of anthropology professor Douglas Caulkins and of the Ethnographic Research Methods students who conducted the interviews with graduating seniors.

Chapter 7
A Mixed Methods Approach to
Assessment in Student Affairs

Lance Kennedy-Phillips
South University

Ellen Meents-DeCaigny
DePaul University

Student affairs divisions have successfully used quantitative and qualitative methods of data collection and analysis. Recently, divisions similar to the Division of Student Affairs at DePaul University have begun collecting and analyzing data using a mixed methods approach. This chapter will provide an example of this type of research and the larger context in which it was conducted.

Introduction

The accountability movement is an active part of management in American higher education. As a result, student affairs divisions have been forced to justify not only their existence as a unit, but also their seat at the table of university decision-making. Divisions across the country have had to devise unique methods of "telling their story" to the university community. In many cases the challenge is to not only show support for the academic mission of the institution, but to also demonstrate responsible stewardship of university resources. Maintaining a culture of evidence built upon consistent data collection will provide the foundation for divisions to assess their contributions to the learning outcomes of the institution.

The problems facing most student affairs organizations are the result of an increase in the rate of change in the environment in which they operate and failure to adapt to such changes.

> *A remarkable number of social and cultural trends, economic forces, population changes, new and emerging technologies, and issues of public policy will have powerful and lasting effects on the ability of colleges and universities to fulfill the demands of their mission and the expectations of their students and constituencies (Keeling, 2004, p. 3).*

Organizations that realize this challenge are moving to strategic management processes to deal proactively with environmental changes.

Strategic management, as defined by Paul Niven, author of *Balanced Scorecard Step-by-Step for Government and Nonprofit Agencies*, is "the use of a process in aligning an organization's short-term activities with long-term goals and success factors" (2002, p. 41).

Collecting data as part of a systematic process increases the accuracy and effectiveness of decision making at both the departmental and divisional level. With the development of a systematic assessment process, data become more reliable. In addition, tracking trends related to divisional key activities helps in the assessment of divisional vitality. Making decisions based on valid data can assist student affairs divisions in securing and allocating resources effectively. In addition, a systematic data collection process can help the division have influence in university policies and decisions.

According to the American Association of Higher Education (2000), assessment is "most effective when it reflects an understanding of organizational outcomes as multidimensional, integrated, and revealed in performance over time" (p. 2). This is accomplished at DePaul by cascading the University's or Student Affair's mission, values, and goals to all levels of the division, aligning budgets and goals to the strategic plan, and using outcomes assessment as a feedback and learning mechanism.

According to Askew and Ellis (2005), strategic thinking should "be the passion, heart and soul of today's student affairs professional whether entry-level staff member, mid-level manager, or senior administrator" (p. 10). Thus, strategic thinking comprises those decisions that are concerned with the entire environment in which the institution or division operates. The DePaul University model involves all levels of the division and challenges each staff member to contribute to its success. Initiating an assessment process around the principles of strategic management ensures that the departments in the division are involved in the day-to-day process of achieving their goals and meeting the factors that lead to the success of the division.

In January 2003, the Student Affairs Division at DePaul University engaged the university community in a process to define and shape the "DePaul Student Experience." As a result, the division developed a long-range strategic plan that included an integrative assessment initiative. The process was designed to measure the day-to-day operations of the division, as well as the division's impact on student learning, engagement, and involvement.

To move the initiative forward, the Division of Student Affairs, in conjunction with the Office of Institutional Planning and Research and the Office of Teaching, Learning, and Assessment, developed an assessment process that incorporated the principles of strategic management and program assessment. The purpose of this process is to develop a culture of evidence to support the decision-making processes of the division and the university. The three overarching goals of the assessment initiative are to focus on data-driven decision making, to promote continuous improvement, and to understand how the division contributes to student learning. Using the division's mission as a guide, the division department chairs determined critical environmental factors that needed to be in place to support student success at DePaul. These critical factors are referred to as *success factors* and constitute programs, services and collaborations that support the mission of the division. The 14 departments in Student Affairs each contribute to some subset of the success factors.

The Model

In an effort to address the growing need for accountability at the university and departmental level, the Division of Student Affairs at DePaul University developed a process they believe addresses good practices of assessment in higher education and the use of strategic management principles. This process provides a clear articulation of the impact student affairs programs have on the fulfillment of the institution's mission. The division can no longer rely on anecdotal decision-making; decisions need to be made based on data collected as part of a systematic and systemic process. The data provide the context to understand the effectiveness of programs and services offered by the division. Members of the division receive training regarding how to collect student learning outcomes data quantitatively, qualitatively, and through the use of mixed methods. These data enhance the discourse regarding what students are learning and add to the culture of evidence.

An effective assessment model supports a cascading process that considers the mission of the university, division, and each department. The development of key activities at all levels of the organization allows for clear and consistent establishment of resource allocation and program development decisions. With the collection of data to support the key activities of each department and the overall division, a culture of evidence is developed that assesses student learning and program performance over time. The goal of this process is to collect evidence that demonstrates the viability of programs developed and sponsored by the Division of Student Affairs (Exhibit 1). In addition, this process allows the members of the division to share their story with the greater community.

The DePaul process measures the environment, the activities, and the outcomes associated with those activities for the division. The environmental measures allow the division to understand its position in the institution and with peer institutions, relative to the mission and vision it has established. The goal of the process is to provide a framework to translate the mission and goals of the division into operational terms, or key activities.

The success factors (Exhibit 2) were developed after a review of the key activities of each department. The key activities represent the day-to-day operations of the department and serve as the framework for measuring

Exhibit 1
Integrated Assessment Model

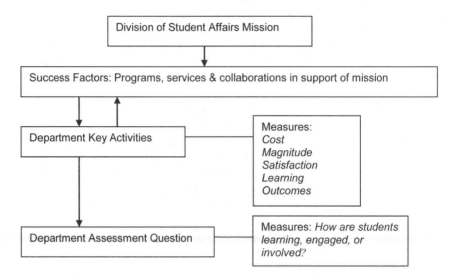

departmental performance throughout the academic year. Key activities are measured according to cost, magnitude, satisfaction, and learning outcomes. Cost measures include but are not limited to: cost per student; cost per staff; overhead; and all expenditure used in support of a particular activity. Magnitude measures the impact of the activity on the university community. This number can be stated as sum, average or ratio. Satisfaction measures the ability of the activity to meet not only the expectations of the participants in the activity, but also satisfaction of the learning outcomes associated with the activity. Each activity is grounded in a set of learning outcomes. The learning outcomes ensure that the activities of the departments are supporting the learning enterprise of the institution.

The key activities are the essential functions of the department and division that lead to fulfillment of the division's mission. It is critical for each department of the division to clearly articulate key activities and the measures that demonstrate progress towards fulfilling those activities. This process results in the development of an annual report of key activities by each department, which contributes to the identification of divisional success factors. The key activities represent the everyday management processes for the department. A vast majority of the division's data-driven evidence is captured in the measurement of the key activities.

Each department and the division decide on one assessment question to answer for the year. The assessment question is derived from the learning outcomes developed for the key activities. The process has to be

Exhibit 2
Divisional Success Factors

The following is a description of the success factors. Base-line data for each success factor has been collected in 2004-2005 to be used as comparative data for future years.

1. Quality Programs constitute co-curricular and extra-curricular learning opportunities that support students' transformational learning and foster students' personal growth and development. Quality programs include new student orientation, leadership workshops, diversity workshops, involvement in student organizations, Residential Education programs, Cultural Center programs, spiritual development opportunities social justice and civic engagement programs, skill development workshops, health and wellness programs, and Life Skills workshops.

2. Intervention and Support Services are provided to students on a one-on-one or structured group basis to enhance their educational experiences by removing barriers to their success. Advocacy, tutoring, advising, counseling, and crisis management are examples of intervention and support services.

3. Community Service activities engage students and the university community in service experiences with and for external constituencies in need. Service experiences include service days, immersion trips, service organizations, student organization philanthropy projects, and departmental service projects.

4. Staff Training and Development is designed to develop skills, abilities and awareness around a particular position. It is also intended to assist with preparation for future professional positions and to foster upward mobility. Staff training is divided into three groups of individuals within the division: student/paraprofessionals (resident advisors, STARS mentors, orientation mentors, DSCA coordinators, etc.), graduate assistants/interns/externs, and professional staff.

5. University Celebrations foster pride, build school spirit and connect students to the larger DePaul community. Annual celebrations fall into four categories: cultural appreciation (Martin Luther King Prayer Breakfast, President's Diversity Brunch, Festival of Lights, etc.), leadership recognition (Arthur J. Schmitt Awards Ceremony, Egan Hope Scholars Ceremony, Senior Leadership Awards Ceremony, departmental year-end ceremonies, etc.), religious ceremonies (Mass of the Holy Spirit, Baccalaureate Mass, weekly liturgy, *etc.*) and social events (Blue Demon Days, Homecoming, Fest, etc.).

6. University Partnerships are an essential element of the Student Affairs division. Developing and implementing effective programs and supporting student success requires the work of many. Collaboration occurs across the division and is structured according to immediacy, student need, impact and relation to long-term and short-term divisional goals. While there are numerous examples of effective partnerships, such as the Loop Development Task Force, the Student Welfare Task Force and the University Center of Chicago Taskforce.

manageable and answering one assessment question is appropriate for this process. A deterrent to progress is attempting to measure more than is possible. The developers of the model believe an assessment process that is too complicated will eventually lead to the failure of the process. Each year the department can choose to assess a different aspect of their program or continue answering the assessment question from the previous year, if it is warranted. The methodology for the assessment project depends on the proposed question.

All data sources are considered when measuring the division's impact on student learning, engagement, and involvement. Quantitative data are collected through intake forms, budget documents, and surveys. Qualitative data are collected through focus groups, interviews, written documents, and professional observation. As demonstrated in our case study, some departments use a mixed methods approach that incorporates both qualitative and quantitative methodologies to collect and analyze data. There is little argument about the value of assessment and the collection of data that demonstrate the impact of our programs on student learning. The question of what should be measured and how that information should be used has been more problematic (Ruben, 1999). In addition, practitioners struggle with the appropriate methodology for conducting assessment of student learning. In what circumstances should we use a quantitative methodology versus a qualitative methodology? When should we use both?

Quantitative methods are recommended if departments are attempting to use a descriptive, comparative, or correlative approach to collect assessment data (McMillan, 2000). Descriptive research includes studies that provide information about frequency or amount of time spent during a particular activity. Comparative studies examine differences between groups on a particular variable or subject. Correlative studies, on the other hand, investigate the relationship between two or more variables. For example, a department could attempt to determine if there is a correlation between an activity of the department and student retention.

McMillan (2000) defines qualitative research as "a phenomological model in which multiple realities are rooted in the subjects' perceptions. A focus on understanding and meaning is based on verbal narratives and observations rather than numbers" (p. 10). Because of its exploratory nature, qualitative research is a popular methodology with departments within the Division of Student Affairs at DePaul University. Departments are able to get a deeper understanding the guiding assessment question. Departments use focus groups, document analysis, and professional observation to answer questions regarding the department's impact on student learning.

The data from mixed methods research provide a rich source for measuring the environment. As the case study will demonstrate, some departments combine qualitative and quantitative paradigms into a mixed research methods approach. According to Johnson and Onwuegbuzie, "the goal of mixed methods research is to maximize the strengths and minimize the weaknesses of [qualitative and quantitative methods] in a single research study" (2004, p. 15). Departments that strive to gain a deeper understanding of their proposed assessment question find the mixed methods approach to be beneficial. In this particular case study, the department implemented a mixed methods approach that used the results of a survey instrument to develop questions for focus group interviews to further understand the quantitative data.

The Case Study

The division's assessment process is grounded in two central questions: how do our programs and services impact student learning; and how can we share that information with the broader community? Each department within the division develops an annual assessment plan to indirectly address these questions by posing an assessment question directly tied to one of the department's key activities. For University Ministry (the focus of our case study) these key activities include facilitating opportunities and activities (Catholic, community service, interfaith/ecumenical), and providing pastoral counseling and support. These key activities are reflective of the department's mission.

As a part of the annual assessment process, the University Ministry staff reviewed their four key activities and chose community service (see Exhibit 3) as their area of focus. Within community service, there are six areas: (a) university service days; (b) on-going student organization service activities (DCSA); (c) service immersion trips; (d) the Vincent and Louise House; (e) the Faith and Civic Engagement Project; and (f) other one-day service events. After considering what area and aspect of service they were most interested in exploring, the department decided to study the impact of service immersion trips. The department decided to study students who participated in service immersion trips and explore what they had learned as a result of their experience. The department determined that a mixed methods approach would provide a more comprehensive perspective of student learning.

Methodology and Results

Silverman (2000) warns researchers to be cautious when choosing a mixed methods approach: "Often the desire to use multiple methods arises because (researchers) want to get at many different aspects of a phenomenon, however, this may mean that (they) have not yet narrowed down (their) topic" (p. 50). University Ministry, however, was confident that a mixed methods approach would allow them to look at different aspects of the same phenomenon. Pairing pre- and post-trip surveys with follow-up focus groups was an attractive option. The rationale for this approach was that surveys could help determine change over time, and focus groups would

Exhibit 3
Example of Key Activity Report

University Ministry
Key Activity #2: Community Service

Cost:
Staff: 4 Full-time Staff (100% of time)
                  1 Assistant Director (75% of time)
Student Leaders - compensated:
            DCSA Senior leaders (3), Service Immersion
                  Programs Student Coordinator (1),
            DCSA Group Leaders (30)
Operational Budget Costs (direct): $41,000
Operational Budget Costs (indirect): $12,000

Magnitude:
University Service Days (3)
            1,725 Students, staff, faculty, and community
                  members
            7,475 hours of community service
DePaul Community Service Associations (DCSA)
            200 Students participate weekly x 30 weeks
            10,300 hours of community service performed
Service Immersions
            14 service trips
            127 students participated
            2,000 hours of service performed
Vincent & Louise House
            10 Students participate for one year
            1,800 hours of service performed
            Weekly communal formation/education meetings
FACE Project (Faith and Civic Engagement)
            10 Faith and Civic Engagement dialogues with 219
                  student participants
Community Service: Other
            Educational Programs (15 programs totaling 1,338
                  participants)
            VIA Reflections (40 sessions, 20 repeat participants
                  at each)
            Retreats (1 DCSA Retreat, 36 participants)

Satisfaction:
1. Immersion Trips: Student leader journal, staff mentor journal, trip participant evaluation, site evaluations, assessment project
2. Service Days: Volunteer participant evaluation card
3. DCSA: Weekly check-ins, DCSA group/site quarterly evaluation
4. Amate: 1 on 1 meeting, participant evaluation of experience
5. Professional observation for all activities
6. The Louise Project Evaluation Form and Satisfaction Survey

Learning Outcomes:
1. Increase leadership ability of students in relation to faith-based service.
2. Engage volunteers in UMIN created reflection on service to ensure that learning and meaning are tied to all service.
3. Make connection for volunteers between Vincentian and Catholic mission of University and faith-based service and Catholic Social Teaching.

allow for in-depth exploration of specific topics related to the student learning experience. This rationale is supported by the work of Johnson and Onwuegbuzie (2004) in their article entitled, "Mixed Methods Research: A Research Paradigm Whose Time has Come." Johnson and Onwuegbuzie believe a mixed method design can be superior to a mono-method design in that qualitative methods, such as focus groups, can serve as a "way to discuss directly the issues under investigation and tap into the participants' perspectives and meanings" that may be missed using an experimental (quantitative) model (p. 18-19).

While the broader assessment question addressed student learning, the department was particularly interested in students' knowledge of their assigned service sites and general attitudes and behaviors related to service and serving others. To further focus the project, the methodology was designed to probe into the impact of the experience relative to the five foundational tenets of the service immersion program: service, simple living, social justice, intentional community, and spirituality (See Exhibit 4, pg. 98).

Survey questions were developed to address three constructs regarding service: students' knowledge, attitudes, and behaviors. Questions were organized according to what Suskie calls, "a natural flow both logically and psychologically" (1996 p. 60). The survey included 3 demographic questions and 20 statements to which students were asked to respond using a Likert scale of strongly agree to strongly disagree (See Exhibit 5, pg. 100).

After students were selected to participate in the service immersion program, they were assigned to one of nine service locations. Students and

Exhibit 4
University Ministry Service Immersion Program Philosophy

The five tenets of the University Ministry Community Service Immersion Program draw upon the lives of Saints Vincent DePaul and Louise deMarillac. They are: service, spirituality, social justice, intentional living, and community.

Service: Service is the cornerstone of the service immersion program at DePaul. In the spirit of Vincent DePaul, serving people on the margins is an essential act of solidarity. The goal is to nourish the inherent human dignity of all persons through the mutual sharing of time, talent and resources. The specific type of service depends on the needs of the host community. All immersions strive to embody a philosophy of service that celebrates the balance of "doing" the work of service and building relationships by "being" with the people we serve.

Spirituality: The philosophy behind this tenet is two-fold. First, service without reflection is just work. Reflection is necessary in order to better understand the complexity of the issues that people on the margins face in their daily lives. Therefore, each night the DePaul community will gather to reflect on the day. These discussions provide opportunities for participants to process their experience and learn from one another. Second, What motivates you? The service immersion program upholds the sacred-ness of all life. In each experience, students are challenged to look deeply at their own lives and source for living. For Vincent DePaul and Louise de Marillac, their service with the poor was rooted in the person of Jesus Christ. Whether or not you come from a religious background or specific faith tradition, the service immersion experience will challenge each participant to look more deeply at his/her motivating source and life values.

Intentional Community: Each community will consist of DePaul students and a staff/faculty mentor. The purpose of building intentional community is to provide a unique opportunity for students to create a shared lifestyle, one that emphasizes human dignity and the common good. Central to this tenet is the Vincentian value that individuals come together in community to support one another in their work.

Simplicity: Living with intention is meant to help students heighten their awareness of the issues of access, availability, and allocation of resources. It is also an opportunity to live in solidarity with the people of the host community. This process can begin to shape one's short- and long-term decisions about how to spend resources of time, talent and money. In community, the students define their common lifestyle by making consensus decisions about food purchases, recycling, technology usage, etc. The commitment is more than attempting to live within a budget or to feel deprived of favorite things. It is a shift of focus. Spending an immersion centered less on money and the consumption promoted by our American culture can free students to experience the value of simple pleasures, conversations, and their own creativity. [1]

Social Justice: The reason for living intentionally, in community, serving others is to strive for social justice. Much of the disparity of resource allocation and marginalization results from systemic injustice. The purpose of this tenet is to increase one's awareness of the unjust political, economic, and social structures which impinge upon the human dignity of people. Students are challenged to explore the causes and effects of injustice whereby they can begin to understand their role in creating a more just world.

[1] Excerpts taken from the Jesuit Volunteer Corps Web site.

trip leaders then met a total of four times prior to their departure. It is during the second pre-trip meeting that students were asked to complete a pre-trip survey. The pen and paper survey was administered by the staff member leading the trip.

At the end of the service trip, students completed the survey a second time, either on-site at their service location or in the van as they drove back to the university. Both settings allowed for immediate feedback regarding the experience and provided a common group setting in that the groups were still intact and immersed in the experience.

The results of the survey then informed the development of focus group questions.

According to Silverman (2000), "'Mapping' one set of data upon another is a more or less complicated task depending on your analytical framework" (p. 51). In particular, Silverman (2000) warns researchers about looking at a single 'phenomenon' when using data collected in one context and comparing it to data collected in another context. While the department recognized the possible limitations of comparing survey results and focus group responses, the primary intention was to use the survey results as a baseline for understanding student learning in relation to the three constructs and five tenets. Since the survey results were used to determine which areas of student learning would be further explored in a focus group setting, the timing of the quantitative and qualitative phases of this study was an important element of the mixed methods approach (Johnson & Onwuegbuzie, 2004).

Exhibit 5
Spring Break Service Immersion Trips

Student Participant Pre/Post Survey

On which Spring Break Service Immersion are you participating / did you participate? (a list of sites was provided)

Have you participated in a service immersion at DePaul University before Spring Break 2006? _____ Year in school: _____

For each statement below, please indicate your <u>current</u> level of agreement or disagreement by placing and "X" in the appropriate box:

#	Statements	Strongly Disagree	Disagree	Neutral	Agree	Strongly Agree	Not Applicable
1	I know about the city / location where my service immersion was held						
2	I know about the issue/s addressed by my service immersion's learning focus/issue (theme of immersion; see listing above)						
3	I know about the population group that I served on my service immersion						
4	I felt comfortable with the population group being served on my service immersion						
5	I participate in regular community service opportunities as a student at DePaul						
6	I have a strong self-knowledge and understanding						
7	It is important to me to have a regular faith practice that sustains me and my values/commitments (e.g. prayer/meditation)						
8	Service to others is an important value to me						

#	Statements	Strongly Disagree	Disagree	Neutral	Agree	Strongly Agree	Not Applicable
9	It is important to me to use my resources wisely (financial, material, personal)						
10	I understand the Catholic, Vincentian and urban mission of DePaul						
11	I am interested or curious about social justice issues						
12	I am interested or curious about spirituality						
13	I make decisions in my life based on my desire to live a more simple lifestyle						
14	I feel engaged in the Catholic, Vincentian and urban mission of DePaul						
15	I am thoughtful and discerning about how I use my resources (financial, material, personal)						
16	I feel compelled to act on behalf of those who are in need or who suffer injustice						
17	I take action on behalf of others who are in need or who suffer injustice						
18	I value a sense of community and understand its importance in my life						
19	I want to make changes in my life in order to better integrate my day to day lifestyle and choices with the things that I value and believe to be important						
20	Integrating faith/spirituality into my life is important to me						

Please explain/comment as needed on any of the above.

Exhibit 6
Focus Group Protocol

Department Name: University Ministry

Time:

Date:

Place:

Moderator:

Note-taker:

Grand Tour Question: What have students learned as a result of their participation in University Ministry Service Immersion Trips (Spring 2006)?

Focus Group Questions:
1) What were your expectations for the service immersion trip experience? Were your expectations met? Why or why not?

2) Are there ways in which you've changed as a result of the experience?

3) Since you've returned are there specific choices you've made differently in your life based on your experience? Please be concrete.

4) Has your understanding of social justice changed as a result of your experience?

5) Did the focus on simple living during the immersion trip impact you in any way (upon your return to campus)?

6) Based upon your immersion experience has there been any change in the way you think about or integrate your faith or spirituality into your life?

7) Was there anything else that you took away from the experience that we haven't discussed?

The survey results indicated an increase in student knowledge regarding the site and populations served during their trips. Specifically, students reported that they were more knowledgeable about their city destination, the issue or theme of their particular trip, and the population they served. In addition, the survey results indicated a shift in students' feelings of engagement in the mission of the University. Lastly, the survey results did not indicate a measurable change in students' attitudes or behaviors related to three of the five tenets: faith or spirituality, simple living, and social justice.

Based on the results of the survey, the department decided to further explore students' learning in the areas of spiritual growth, simple living, and social justice. To do so, the department intentionally designed focus group questions related to these tenets (See Exhibit 6).

All service trip participants were invited to participate in one of two focus groups during the tenth week of the quarter. Of the 55 students invited, 9 chose to participate. The low participation rate could be due to the calendar, as the interviews were scheduled during exam week. Each focus group included a facilitator and note taker not affiliated with the department. The focus groups lasted approximately 60 minutes and were audio taped.

Based on the handwritten notes and audiotapes, the focus group facilitator provided the department a summary of responses to each focus group question. University Ministry staff members then conducted a qualitative analysis of these notes and developed five overall themes that emerged from the students' statements. Themes that emerged included: a greater understanding of the connection between faith and social justice; stronger appreciation of their own privilege (gratitude); a greater and more personal understanding of the experience of the poor; and a deeper questioning of materialism within the U.S. culture and a desire to live a simpler lifestyle.

Using a mixed methods approach, the department was able to piece together a more comprehensive picture of student learning related to the service immersion experience. Students' knowledge of service sites and the populations served was uncovered through survey data, while information regarding students' general attitudes and behaviors related to service, specifically in the areas of spiritual growth, simple living, and social justice, was uncovered through focus group data.

In addition to what the department learned about the impact of service immersion trips on student participants, the key take-away from the assessment project was the need to better attend to and support the re-integration of students into the university community after they return from a service immersion trip. This finding was uncovered during the focus groups, particularly in response to the last question; Was there anything else that you took away from the experience that we haven't discussed? Students shared that they felt lonely when they returned and struggled to re-connect with family and friends when wanting to share their experience. As a way to assist them in their transition, students suggested more structured opportunities to process the experience after returning. While University Ministry did not expect to uncover this information about the program, the candid feedback and suggestions for program improvement have been taken seriously and will be used to inform future decisions.

It is important to not only assess key program outcomes, but to use data to inform decisions regarding changes to the program and to implement changes in a timely fashion. In this case, service immersion trips play a key role in fulfilling the Division of Student Affair's commitment to community service and the University's commitment to serving others. The success of this program impacts the success of the department, the division, and the larger institution. Therefore, positive changes to the program can potentially "cascade" upward and have a positive effect on all three levels of the institution.

The department will use the assessment data to drive program improvement. For example, the department plans to restructure the immersion experience by adding opportunities for students to better re-integrate into the campus community following the immersion trip. The goal is to reduce students' feelings of isolation, support students as they strive to make sense of their experience, and encourage continued involvement in community service. A residual effect of this change might be an increase in student involvement in community service which could further strengthen students' feelings of engagement in the university's mission.

Lessons Learned

There are multiple lessons to be learned from this assessment project and the use of a mixed methods approach. First, conducting research of this nature can provide professional development opportunities for professional staff in student affairs. Second, designing, collecting, and analyzing data with a mixed research method takes time and resources from a department. Third, there is value in using a mixed methods approach when assessing student learning in a student affairs setting. Fourth, a sound research design is critical to the success of the assessment process. Finally, being open-minded and listening to participants' stories can lead to unexpected findings that drive program improvement.

At the department level, student affairs staff members can increase their capacity to conduct assessment by learning to design and implement surveys and focus groups, as well as analyze both qualitative and quantitative data. "Multiple methods are tempting because they seem to give you a fuller picture. However, you need to be aware that multiple sources of data mean that you will have to learn many more data analysis skills" (Silverman, 2000, p. 50). In the case of University Ministry, understanding the results of the surveys was the first challenge. Using the survey results to create focus group questions to further explore student learning was a second challenge. A third challenge was analyzing the focus group data and linking the findings to the survey data. Fortunately, University Ministry received assistance in addressing these challenges from the Student Affairs Assessment and Research Coordinator who was available throughout the process to help facilitate and provide training regarding the analysis of data.

Practitioners should consider time and resources when designing a methodology. Focus groups can produce rich data and meaningful stories that help the department understand its impact on the population studied. However, departments need to strategically plan for the time it takes to develop focus group questions, coordinate focus group meetings, and solicit participation. In the case of University Ministry, the focus groups were intentionally facilitated 8 to 10 weeks after the immersion experience to allow participants time to reflect on their experience. The challenge, however, is that the university operates on a quarter system, which means that the focus groups took place the week before final exams. The department spent considerable time contacting and reminding students to participate in order to ensure attendance.

In addition to the time it takes to design assessment instruments and facilitate the process, time has to be allocated to conduct a thorough analysis. Depending on the method of analysis, it takes time to structure the analysis. For example, the decision to collect data via a pen and paper survey can add additional steps to the analysis process in that the participant responses have to be organized and entered into a data (*i.e.*, Excel or Access) spreadsheet before being analyzed. The analysis of qualitative data also takes time. Whether the group decides to use a use a pen-and-paper method of coding the documents or utilize text analysis software, both methods require additional time for training and analysis.

During a mixed methods approach there is an additional step to the analysis. Not only did the department analyze the qualitative and quantitative data, it had to compare the results of both methods and determine a final analysis. Because this is a complex methodology that requires expertise in quantitative and qualitative methods, departments or divisions should not hesitate to ask for assistance from other areas, such as institutional research or academic areas (*i.e.*, sociology, psychometrics, anthropology, *etc.*). The experts, if not conducting the study, can provide training and or consultation to novice researchers. This is a critical lesson to learn. The stronger the design of the study, the more impact the study will likely have on decision making.

Another lesson learned was the value of using a mixed methods approach. In the case of University Ministry, having solid outcomes and tenets to work with were important in developing both the survey and focus group questions. The tenets, particularly, helped structure the focus group questions. The survey could capture information regarding increased knowledge or basic level changes in attitudes and behaviors, but the focus groups allowed for in-depth exploration of more complex topics such as simple living, social justice, and spirituality.

A final lesson learned was the importance of being open to uncovering the unexpected. Conducting assessment can be a risky process since it is uncertain as to what students will say about a department's programs and services. In the case of University Ministry, one of the key findings came from an open-ended question asked at the end of each focus group: Was there anything else that you took away from the experience that we haven't discussed? As a result of this question the department learned that the program was successful in having a powerful impact on students, however, the experience left students feeling isolated and unsure how to communicate what they learned to friends and family. Because University Ministry was willing to take a risk and ask a question whose answer they did not know, they were able to collect rich data that will help drive program improvement.

References

American Association for Higher Education (AAHE) (2000). *Principles of good practice for assessing student learning.* Washington, DC: American Association of Higher Education.

Askew, P., & Ellis, S. (2005, Spring). The power of strategic planning. *NASPA Leadership Exchange, (pp. 5-8).*

Johnson, R. B., & Onwuegbuzie, A. J. (2004, October). Mixed methods research: A research paradigms whose time has come. *Educational Researcher, 33*, (7), (pp. 14–26).

Keeling, R. (Ed.). (2004). *Learning reconsidered: A campus-wide focus on the student experience.* Washington, DC: National Association of Student Personnel Administrators & American College Personnel Association. http://www.naspa.org/membership/leader_ex_pdf/lr_long.pdf (Active as of 2/28/07)

McMillian, J. H. (2000). *Educational research: Fundamentals for the consumer* (3rd ed.). New York: Longman.

Niven, P. R. (2002). *Balanced scorecard step-by-step for government and nonprofit agencies.* New York: Wiley.

Ruben, B. D. (1999). *Toward a balanced scorecard for higher education: Rethinking the college and university excellence indicators framework.* Baltimore: The Hunter Group.

Silverman, D. (2000). *Doing qualitative research: A practical handbook.* London: Sage Publications Ltd.

Suskie, L. A., (1996). *Questionnaire survey research: What works* (2nd ed.). Tallahassee, FL: Association for Institutional Research.

Chapter 8
Mixed Methods and Strategic Planning

Richard A. Voorhees
Principal, Voorhees Group LLC

Introduction

Without skillful use of mixed methodologies, most strategic planning processes would fall far short of their lofty intentions. Organizations, especially higher education organizations, are complex. Understanding where best to advance strategy requires multiple points of intelligence gathering coupled with an understanding of how an institution's interactions shape its capability to pursue that strategy. Interactions that shape a college or university occur along formal and informal pathways both internally and externally. Capturing and understanding quantitative and qualitative indicators throughout the strategic planning process, including those indicators that emerge along multiple pathways as the process unfolds, can spell the difference between a meaningful strategic plan and one that gathers dust. Drawn from the author's experience in facilitating strategic plans in higher education institutions, this chapter illustrates how both quantitative and qualitative methods can be combined to create meaningful directions for an institution's future.

At its most basic, strategic planning is a process of anticipating change, identifying new opportunities, and executing strategy. Strategic planning can also be described as idea management in which new ideas are developed (or brainstormed), categorized, processed, and implemented. It is a journey that begins best when appropriate data, drawn from multiple sources and using multiple techniques, are transformed into "actionable" information. Contrasted to "pedestrian information," actionable information makes obvious the next steps an institution should consider. For example, understanding that an institution's enrollment is increasing is, for the most part, routine knowledge across a campus. Understanding what market segments are growing and the institution's penetration rate of those segments helps the institution to understand what actions may be needed to manage that growth. Ideally, the availability of actionable information creates an expanded appetite for more actionable information. Skillful uses of mixed methods are critical for institutions seeking to harvest the best possible actionable information to guide strategy. Employing quantitative and qualitative methods interdependently, and in balance, can mean the difference between true strategy or strategy that only "seems right."

Quantitative and Qualitative Techniques
Applied to Strategic Planning

Quantitative and qualitative paradigms make different contributions to strategic planning. The quantitative paradigm helps strategic planners to describe the "what" in an organization while the qualitative paradigm can answer "why" it is happening. In general, qualitative methods provide a better understanding of the context in which the development of institutional strategy can occur. Quantitative methodologies, on the other hand, provide an assessment of how the institution is currently functioning. The interest in qualitative techniques to supplement what has traditionally been perhaps an overreliance on quantitative measures appears to be accelerating in recent years (National Science Foundation, 1997).

As used in this chapter, qualitative methodology refers broadly to human interactions and how data gathered from those interactions can guide the development of strategy. Included here are one-on-one interviewing, focus groups, and what the author terms, "strategy sessions." Information gathered using these techniques can be used to guide the collection of additional quantitative data. More importantly, however, qualitative data should be used to make intelligent, informed decisions about what types of strategic actions an institution can reasonably pursue. Quantitative methods, as their name implies, are chiefly techniques that use numbers to indicate an institution's operation and its environment. Included in this chapter are quantitative techniques such as accessing and examining internal and external databases, constructing and analyzing questionnaires, and the construction of Geographical Information System (GIS) maps.

A successful model for strategic planning incorporates both quantitative and qualitative data collection in a symbiotic way. Tashakkori and Teddlie (2003) suggest three temporal sequences for combining quantitative and qualitative data: (a) concurrently, in which two types of data are collected and analyzed in parallel, (b) sequentially, in which one type of data provides a basis for collection of another type of data, and (c) conversion, where the data are "qualitized" or "quantitized" and analyzed again. Taken together, there are primary and secondary uses for these techniques as they are applied to specific elements of strategic planning as discussed later in this chapter. As Howard notes in the introduction to this volume, decisions that researchers make about when to employ quantitative and qualitative choices are not always based on the question at hand; occasionally this choice is based on pragmatic realities including available resources and time. The case study presented below illustrates these dynamics.

A Case Study

Among the largest community colleges in the United States, Broward Community College (BCC or Broward) is a multi-campus college district comprising three large campuses and three educational centers. Located in South Florida and stretching 25 miles north to south and 50 miles east to west, Broward County consists of 30 municipalities and almost 1,200 square miles. Only the eastern portion (410 square miles) is developed, however. This area is nearly at capacity for development, a fact that drives land and housing values upward. Palm Beach County lies to the north and Miami-Dade County to the south. The Atlantic Ocean marks the County's east border.

Under direction of a new president and to respond to expectations by its regional accrediting body, BCC embarked on a strategic planning process in 2004. The Education Master Plan, as it is known at Broward, has become the guiding force for strategic management and the framework for operational planning across all units of the College. To accomplish this, a deliberate process was launched to engage internal and external stakeholders in identifying key decisions facing the College and by harvesting actionable data. The process began in that fall and culminated in a report to the College community in the spring of 2005.[1] This experience is used in this chapter to illustrate how mixed methodologies can converge to produce a strategic plan. Although the institutional type portrayed here is a community college, the techniques illustrated below and the lessons learned from employing mixed methodologies within these techniques can be instructive to all institutions that embark on strategic planning.

Strategic Planning Elements and Mixed Methods

Each of the elements used to create the Broward strategic plan are discussed below. Readers will note considerable overlap among these elements as well as the synergy between qualitative and quantitative methodologies within each planning element.

Environmental Scan

Broadly put, a scan of an institution's environment requires not just a volume of information but, at the first level of analysis, the ability to discern within that information what is critical to the development of that institution's strategy. Data for environmental scanning are abundant and are growing more so on the Internet. Much of these data, however, fall short of criteria for inclusion in an environmental scan because they lack a direct connection to the institution or because their reliability are questionable. Before they can be helpful, their connection to the institution's scope of operation needs to be established. A second level of analysis, therefore, requires knowledge of the institution's current operations—a knowledge that can most quickly be gained by talking with key faculty and staff, in other words, qualitative interviewing.

While most of the activity generated in compiling a meaningful environmental scan may appear to be a simple act of data retrieval and quantitative analysis, no scan can exist independently of an institution's organizational structure and the culture that drives that structure. Learning about that culture and structure requires skillful use of qualitative techniques including individual interviews, group interviews, and tabulating the interview data. These data create a framework that can be used to diagnosis the institution's current strategic stance and capability to pursue strategic actions. The results of the environmental scan were used as the basis for creating protocols for individual interviews and strategy sessions.

Interviewing Key Stakeholders

Skillful interviews yield helpful qualitative information. A solid foundation for these interviews can be set by a thorough review of quantitative characteristics of the institution. In general, the more that the interviewer prepares for these interviews—the deeper that she or he understands basic institutional data—the better information the interviews will yield. Once that framework is clear in the interviewer's mind, the next step is to establish rapport with the interviewee. While quantitative data indicate the extent to which outcomes are being met, qualitative interviews speak more to how the participants feel about what is happening within an institution. Since mobilizing participants is key to future actions, a deep understanding of their perceptions advances the strategic planning agenda. Preparing for interviews mobilized key stakeholders at BCC since they felt that they were not being interviewed "cold."

The results of qualitative interviews themselves may point to uncovering sources of an institution's quantitative data or to offering new meaning for that data. To ensure that those conversations yield maximum return, it always is recommended that the preparation for interviews with key stakeholders—a qualitative process—-be augmented by analyses of existing institutional data resulting from quantitative processes. Careful structuring of these interviews ensures that actionable data are captured from a wide variety of sources.

Focus Groups

The term *focus group* has taken on multiple meanings in higher education. It has been used to describe casual conversations with more than several people in random settings, a misuse of the term. More appropriately, a focus group is a deliberate event planned to gather specific information. Well-planned and executed focus groups are a qualitative exercise involving a protocol of questions designed to elicit communication without circumscribing meaningful dialogue. In the same way that the preparation for one-on-one interviews requires intimate knowledge of the institution to be effective, focus group preparation requires the interviewee to understand the underlying issues facing the institution's strategic planning process initially and how to understand participant perspectives of those issues can serve as a test bed for examination of the issues.

Because higher education institutions are typically very busy places, creating focus groups is difficult, especially if they are based on participants' affiliation with the institution. Separate focus groups scheduled for students, administrators, and community stakeholders may not only be difficult to organize, they may also produce low attendance. Further, if it is intended that focus groups further the strategic planning process by providing an avenue in which participants can learn from one another's perspectives, conducting focus groups based on a participant's relationship with the institution does little to advance that goal. The author's experience holds that focus groups can be helpful for strategic planning, but that heterogeneous groups organized to simultaneously represent the total institution produce deeper communication. Such groups are vertical in an organization, including classified personnel, mid-level managers, faculty, and executive leadership.

Large Group "Strategy Sessions"

Among the most effective strategic planning techniques are large group meetings designed to promote an interchange of ideas about strategic issues facing an organization. Though sometimes labeled as focus groups, their purpose is somewhat different than the definition discussed above. In the author's experience, few stakeholders have been exposed to the concept of actionable data to make meaningful contributions to strategic planning. BCC scheduled 12 strategy sessions to provide maximum access to the strategic planning process. Invitations to participate in the BCC strategy sessions were sent to students, faculty, and administrators to solicit a wide range of perspectives and opinions.

Unlike a focus group in which opinions and perspectives are gathered from participants in a one-way fashion, the facilitator of a strategy session guides a dialogue among the participants about qualitative and quantitative data and how those data combine to produce actionable information for the institution. Carefully designed so that all participants share a foundation of common data, strategy sessions in reality become brainstorming sessions where new ideas can be processed across a range of participants. The sessions began with a presentation of quantitative data about the College's internal and external trends followed by a series of questions developed beforehand, purposefully designed to elicit discussion.

In the author's experience, many strategy session participants will have strong opinions about an institution's future, but not all will share common knowledge about the institution's current functioning as expressed in quantitative terms. A key outcome of strategy sessions is to acquaint participants with data and to explain where those data arise as well as what they mean in predicting the institution's future. Because future strategy depends on credible data, strategy sessions and the process of certifying those data through group processes, played a major role in creating buy-in for the College's strategic plan.

Geographic Information System (GIS) Maps

Most audiences do not react quickly to tabular data, especially if the rows and columns are numerous. Yet, data drawn from census tracts, small statistical subdivisions of a given county, were vital to understanding where BCC might target marketing and recruitment efforts. To make shifts within these tracts easier to digest during the strategy sessions, Geographic Information System (GIS) maps were used to provide a quick, visual overview of population changes, including shifts in income, minority subpopulations, age, and housing values. Constructing these maps was a quantitative activity, driven by software and technology. Interpreting these maps, on the other hand, was a qualitative activity in which interviewees and strategy session participants were asked for their insights on population shifts within the College's service area. For some, this information was fresh; for others the GIS maps produced a new way of looking at BCC's potential student market.

Competitor Analyses

Few institutions are aware of the range of instructional programs available at other institutions with whom they compete for students. This knowledge can be the basis for creating new programs or modifying existing programs. It can also point to programs that might be eliminated. Gathering these data from websites of competitor organizations in proximity to the institution or who compete regionally or nationally in given programs is a basic exercise in tabulating data. However, the nomenclature needed to describe programs so that they can be categorized accurately is learned best from interviewing academic staff and faculty. Program titles may not match their content, and astute planners will want to ensure that programs that appear, on the surface, to compete with their institution's programs are, in fact, comparable.

Enrollment Forecasting and Scenario Building

The approach used to forecast enrollments for BCC included a baseline, or *status quo*, projection coupled with the development of alternative scenarios based on specific institutional decisions about how to manage future enrollments. This process is decidedly quantitative in nature, especially in the process of constructing projections that compared trends in BCC's market share of key demographics to those corresponding demographics predicted for South Florida. Scenario building, on the other hand, combines the quantitative process of calculating increased market shares with the qualitative process of deciding what specific actions are within the institution's capability to implement. Scenarios developed for BCC included increasing the market share of minority 18 to 24 year-olds first and, then increasing the market share of all 18 to 24 year olds, and finally increasing the market share of 25 to 44 year-olds. The gains for the College in these simulations are considerably larger than the *status quo* baseline projections and led to substantive discussions about the institution's future enrollment mix.

Instructional Program Vitality

The analyses of program enrollment data are yet another strategic exercise that cannot be based on numbers alone. While upward and downward trends in individual programs provide a first place to look when analyzing an institution's instructional menu, the whole story needs to be researched before conclusions are drawn. For example, it may be that enrollments have declined in response to decisions limiting course availability, combining courses across disciplines, faculty retirements, or a lack of program marketing. Each of these potential reasons, and perhaps other considerations, should be balanced against other criteria including shifts in labor markets, expired curriculum that doesn't match current realities, and actions taken, mostly inadvertently, that discourage enrollment. Without knowledge of these factors, gained qualitatively by listening to stakeholders internal and external to the institution, an incomplete picture of program vitality is more than probable.

Internal and External Surveys

One-on-one interviewing and strategy sessions may not substitute for gathering opinions and insights by way of survey research. Data gathered from existing questionnaires and those developed specifically for planning can provide multiple perspectives about a college and its environment. Surveys can be a traditional paper and pencil version or, increasingly, web-based surveys. Survey construction requires knowledge of sampling procedures, reliability issues, and, of course, content validity to ensure that items measure what they purport to measure. Interpreting survey responses is usually regarded as a quantitative activity. Creation of individual survey items that are institutional-specific should ideally be developed from the results of individual interviews, focus groups, and strategy sessions.

Analyses of Labor Market Information

The Internet has made labor market information widely accessible, making it easier for colleges and universities to collect data that can be used to map the connection between the outputs of their career and professional programs and the world of work. Ten-year forecasts are available both for new jobs that will be created and for jobs that will grow most rapidly by county, region, state, and nationally. At the national level, these forecasts are connected to the most significant source of postsecondary education or training required for entry in each occupation forecast.[2]

While employment forecast data are helpful, strategic planners should not expect a perfect fit between job titles and program labels. To provide the best prediction of academic programs requires knowledge not found in external databases. Insights required to accurately estimate the need for programs closely match those insights necessary to gauge program vitality. Interviewing skills and techniques, including the aforementioned need to establish rapport with interviewees as well as guiding the interview, asking appropriate questions about processes, engaging in empathy for the interviewee, and tabulating interview results, are beyond the scope of this chapter, but are key touchstones for ensuring that quantitative data apply to an institution's unique circumstances.

Moving to Operational Planning

Strategic planning often fails to connect the dreams and aspirations that arise in strategic planning to specific actions. While many college and university websites contain visually appealing strategic planning documents, most do not contain specific actions to support the strategy, do not assign responsibility for carrying out those actions, and, do not commit dollars and human resources to make strategic dreams a reality. There is also a tendency to assign responsibility for actions to committees, rather than individuals. Plans of this variety are little more than public relations pieces designed to persuade readers that an institution is carrying out strategy. Mapping the intersection between strategic planning and operational planning and guiding institutions through this process requires finesse in blending mixed methodologies.

The predecessor to the BCC strategic plan described here lacked clear links to operational planning. To close this gap, College administrators asked that specific action strategies be first developed by the consultant to support each of the new nine strategic goals. These initial strategies subsequently were refined in interactions among the College's operational units. The executive decision-making team then identified responsible parties and assigned executive sponsors for each strategy. At this stage of the transition between strategic planning and operational planning, it is very important that potential action strategies not be stated in such global terms that defy measurement. For example, an action strategy statement "improve the educational experience of students" needs more elaboration before it can be measured. On the other hand, a measurement scheme for an action strategy that calls for "improving student success rates in college-level mathematics" is easier to operationalize.

A key role of the consultant in this sub-process was to work with institutional leaders to ensure that the measurement of action strategies were quantifiable so that a clear picture of institutional progress could be made. To this end, the consultant drafted "success factors" to provide a quantitative and qualitative way of assessing goal attainment. These success factors were shared with those responsible for each action strategy and were brought back to the College's cabinet for ratification. This process was iterative and required both a sense of the possible strategies and success factors that the College might pursue as well as an estimation of whether they could reasonably be successful. Some units in the College previously had not considered an accountability system based primarily on success factors. This new system provided a mechanism for those units to engage in deeper conversations with senior administrators about how quantitative and qualitative factors could combine to ensure that progress toward BCC's new strategic goals could be measured.

To further engage each unit in strategic planning and to provide a transparent means of creating potential action strategies and success factors across the entire organization, BCC created an online planning tool. This tool permits a comprehensive overview of the planning process while seeking new quantitative and qualitative data from all layers of the College to inform and potentially improve action strategies and success factors.

Summary of Strategic Planning Elements and Mixed Methodology

Table 1 summarizes the types of mixed methods associated with each of the strategic planning elements discussed above and indicates whether their role is primary or secondary. Note that, in keeping with the symbiotic union between the two techniques, no single strategic planning element is exclusively quantitative nor qualitative.

Improving Strategic Planning through Mixed Methodologies

The application of mixed methodologies as illustrated above is vital to the development of a successful plan and may be helpful for those charged with charting strategy for institutions. From the author's experience several other touchstones for using these techniques may save time and energy in the strategic planning process.

Sharing Techniques and Data

Educating the college community about data sources and the techniques used to harvest those data is an important facet in strategic planning. Explaining data to stakeholders creates credibility for the process, even among the few institutions that have successfully created a culture of inquiry in which quantitative and qualitative data are routinely used to guide decisions. A+ institutions that lack a tradition of either creating or sharing data, strategic planning is likely to make many internal stakeholders uncomfortable, especially if the purpose is to create actionable information. It is critical to the success of strategic planning to establish the credibility for both the techniques employed and the data produced.

Institutions with no quantitative data tradition are also likely to lack the necessary framework in which qualitative data can be helpful to decision making. In fact, when quantitative data are not available, it is certain that

Table 1
Mixed Methodologies and their Application
to Strategic Planning Elements

Primary Methodology	Secondary Methodology	Strategic Planning Application
Quantitative	Qualitative	Environmental Scan
Qualitative	Quantitative	Interviews with Key Stakeholders
Qualitative	Quantitative	Focus Groups
Qualitative	Quantitative	Large Group "Strategy Sessions"
Quantitative	Qualitative	Geographic Information System (GIS) maps
Quantitative	Qualitative	Competitor Analyses
Quantitative	Qualitative	Enrollment Forecasting and Scenario Building
Quantitative	Qualitative	Instructional Program Vitality
Quantitative	Qualitative	Internal and External Surveys
Quantitative	Qualitative	Analyses of Labor Market Information
Qualitative	Quantitative	Creating Action Strategies
Quantitative	Qualitative	Creating Success Factors

previous planning has been based mostly on the opinions of senior administrators. It is also probable that what has previously passed for qualitative data are, in reality, scattered impressions gathered haphazardly. Lack of meaningful quantitative and qualitative data at the onset of the strategic planning process means that considerable effort will be required to position the institution to recognize and incorporate actionable information. The learning curve is steep. It is critical that the process of sharing data where it previously has been unavailable be seen as a first step in this journey.

Planning Cycles

Strategic planning cycles often assume a life of their own. That is, when an institution meets with initial success in strategic planning by demonstrating change through action strategies, it will want to repeat the cycle anew. While continuing the cycle of planning is highly desirable, it is also possible that the institution could become so beholden to the process, and become so busy in animating that process, that it fails to recognize other strategic opportunities. The result is that the purpose of strategic planning, that is, to anticipate, identify, and pursue opportunities, becomes secondary to the institution's planning calendar.

To offset this all-to-common tendency, institutions will want to encourage continuous intelligence gathering while ensuring that the operational planning cycle provides many opportunities to consider fresh information. Updating of environmental scanning should be a routine task. It should incorporate the most recent changes in external quantitative databases as well as the fresh perspectives depicted by qualitative data gathered to support strategic planning including focus groups and interviews with external stakeholders.

Overcoming Amnesia

Strategic planning processes frequently suffer from abandoning previous strategies in favor of strategies that appear to be more attractive. While strategic plans should always be flexible to permit development of new strategic actions, discarding previous action strategies without accounting for their positive contributions to the institution or failures is a fool's errand. To counter memory-free strategy setting, institutions will want to ensure that the previously set success factors attached to each strategy are accurately measured. While it is almost certain that measurement issues will surface when deciding whether a given strategy has met with success, discussion of shortcomings in measurement should not automatically eliminate a strategy from continuation. Rather, there is probably much to be learned about how to improve quantitative and qualitative measurement techniques as applied to institutional strategies that can, in turn, guide new strategies or refine existing strategies.

Providing for Multiple Outcomes

It is far easier to measure the inputs of action strategies than their outputs. Inputs measurements most typically are quantitative and include dollars and human resources allocated to accomplish a given strategy. Measuring the outcomes of action strategies, on the other hand, requires more creativity and a grounding in quantitative and qualitative methodologies. Mixed methods provide a framework for detecting impacts, especially if those impacts are unanticipated or even unintended. Triangulation of data, that is, gathering data from multiple sources and using multiple methods, is always preferred in strategic planning because it ensures that multiple stakeholders can view the process as possessing validity.

Planning Ahead

The desirability of adequate preparation for each strategic planning element mentioned in this chapter has been previously noted. Collection and analysis of actionable data requires initial thought about the suitability of data collection methods as well as how that data will be integrated. First, decisions should be made about the extent to which qualitative methods will be used. They may either provide commentary or provide detailed analyses which can add weight to quantitative data. Second, it is desirable to have a collection schedule and to revisit that schedule throughout the strategic planning process. Early analyses may indicate the need to alter the schedule or technique, including the data sought and whether a switch in primary technique—qualitative or quantitative—is warranted. Periodic revisiting of the schedule can help to mitigate against the strategic planning process becoming overwhelmed by data that is only peripheral.

Summary and Conclusion

This chapter has shown a link between mixed methodologies and effective strategic planning as a desired evolution in strategic planning. Assembling and interpreting quantitative data, in isolation, is no longer a sufficient basis for plotting an institution's future. In an earlier era, when quantitative data were more difficult to gather, chiefly because they were only retrievable in print form, strategic plans with abundant external data were considered state-of-the-art. While there was always a role for qualitative techniques within this generation of strategic planning, extensive use of quantitative data served a larger role in legitimizing the process, especially among external stakeholders.

The next evolution of strategic planning has been ushered in by the Internet and the easy access to data and electronic databases it has provided. While, as discussed earlier, data-free plans still exist, mainly for public relations purposes, there is little justification for strategic planning processes that do not include external quantitative data that are closely matched to the institution's operations and the environment within in which it functions. The relative ease of assembling these data, however, is only a start. It is argued here that unless considerable qualitative acumen is brought to the interpretation and refinement of quantitative data, strategic planning becomes only an exercise that describes "how" without understanding "why." Effective strategic planning today must include a skillful mix of quantitative and qualitative data, both internal and external to the institution, to guide strategy development.

References

National Science Foundation. (1997, August). *User-friendly handbook for mixed method evaluations.* J. Frechtling & L. Sharp (Eds.) Arlington, VA: Author. Retrieved December 11, 2006, at http://www.nsf.gov/pubs/1997/nsf97153/start.htm (active as of 2/6/07)

Tashakkori, A., & Teddlie, C. (Eds.). (2003). *Handbook of mixed methods in social and behavioral research.* Thousand Oaks, CA: Sage Publications.

Endnotes

[1] See Broward Community College Master Plan retrieved December 22, 2006, at http://www.broward.edu/masterplan/presreports.jsp (active as of 2/6/07)

[2] See, for example, the Bureau of Labor Statistics site. http://www.bls.gov/emp emptab3.htm (active as of 2/6/07)